THE REAL BOOK of SHADOWS

PSYCHIC CORDS, DREAM WALKING, SHADOW WORK, SOUL RETRIEVAL & PAST LIFE HEALING

BOOK TWO OF THE SPIRIT WORK SERIES

BY DEBORAH VOITH

About the Author

Deborah Voith is a shamanic witch, a certified traditional Reiki Master-Teacher, and a certified (or maybe certifiable) southern root-worker. She is an intuitive, psychic, and often times a mediumistic tarot reader, who grew up in a haunted house. She has been the purveyor of magical and occult items since 2006 at her shop (formerly brick & mortar, and now online): Bewitchingbee Magical Supply, www.bewitchingbee.com and has taught classes for the past two decades on psychic development, mediumship, witchcraft, reiki, hoodoo root work, tarot and palmistry. She also volunteered as a psychic investigator in a missing person agency. In the past she has been featured in such publications as The Milwaukee Shepherd, and On Milwaukee. She has also been a featured guest on WLIP "The Mothership Connection" and a guest on the Starclear podcast.

Copyright © 2019 Deborah Voith
All rights reserved. No part of this publication may be reproduced in any form without permission from the author.

OTHER BOOKS BY DEBORAH VOITH

Guide to Spirit Communication, with Ancestors, Angels, Spirit Guides, & Allies: Contacting Spirits on the Other Side of the Veil & Beyond. (Book One of the Spirit Work Series) (2019)

Disclaimer: The information provided in this book is given in good faith and is not intended to diagnose any physical or mental condition, nor serve as a substitute for informed medical and/ or psychiatric advice or care. Please contact your health professional for medical and psychological advice or treatment. The author assumes no responsibility for any possible consequences that may result from the readers use and/ or practice of the content contained in this publication and recommends the use of common sense when contemplating or engaging in the practices described in this book.

All herbal formulas within this book are provided for reference. Always check to make sure you have no allergies or sensitivities to the listed ingredients. None of the formulas in this book are meant to be ingested or internally consumed. Herbs and herbal formulas may always pose some risk so caution should always be taken. The author assumes no responsibility for those who choose not to heed this advice.

Please Note: The people and experiences contained within this series of books are true and actual accounts, either of my own or those which were recounted to me by others. Some of the identifying information has been changed to preserve confidentiality.

TABLE OF CONTENTS

Introduction

1. The Energetic Anatomy of Spirit

2. Working with Energy

3. Dream Walking

4. Dream Work

5. Clearing Psychic Debris

6. Dissolving Negative Psychic Cords

7. What is Shadow Work?

8. Visioning into the Shadow

9. Soul Retrieval

10. Exploring & Healing Past Lives

11. In Closing

Bibliography

ACKNOWLEDGEMENTS

First, and always a very special thanks to my husband John, for all his love and support, and to my sister Sharon Blandino, who shares this journey of spirit with me. To my ancestors and my parents Anita and Arthur for bringing me into the world, and to my four adult children Adrian, Justin, Sherene, and Laura for providing me the opportunity to be their mother, and also to my entire family for their patience and support as I worked on this project.

Special shout outs go to all my friends, fellow witches, students, and clients: Jamie Allen (who shares my love of spirit boards!), Heather Adams, Sandy Goronja, Debby Kirn Knoff (my favorite paranormal investigator), and rootworker Michelle Dabrowski for all of her wonderful feedback! A special thanks also goes out to my fellow spirit worker and friend Christopher Lee Jansen for sharing his input and experiences. I would also like to give a big thank you to all of the patrons and customers of my shop, Bewitchingbee Magical Supply, to all of the shamans, witches, magicians, spiritualists, psychics, mediums, ghost hunters, rootworkers, and other seekers who came through the door and shared their experiences, and to all of you who participated in our séances and spirit circles; you all know who you are!

A special thank you to Krystal Stagman and Kyle Hawkshead of Altered State of Mind, and also to John Reeves at House of Magick for inviting me to practice and teach within the very special spaces of their magical shops!

And last, but not least, to all of my helpful ancestors, spiritual teachers, guides, friends, and allies for all of their guidance and help here and on the other side.

Introduction

Do you know anyone who feels stuck in life and unable to move forward? Have you or your family, friends, or a client ever experienced unexplained fears, anxiety, pain, or grief despite consulting with medical professionals? Do you or someone you know feel that they are unable to connect with others or say that it feels like a part of them are missing?

Sometimes the source of these difficulties are related to fragmentation of the self in response to traumatic events, or the development of energetic blockages related to unhealthy psychic cording to another person. When psychic debris or past traumas are unaddressed the damage accumulated in our energetic mental, emotional, and spiritual bodies eventually manifests in our life as physical illness, unresolved chronic anger, fear, or sadness, feeling disconnected, development of a shadow, or may create blockages which are often revealed as an inability to let go of the past or move on to the future.

The Real Book of Shadows will show you how to clear away psychic debris and access the lost parts of self and transform your shadow. With these simple exercises you can guide yourself or another person to heal the inner self through the process of dissolving negative psychic cords or by the journey of Soul Retrieval.

Although this book is mainly written for fellow shamanic witches, spirit workers, and energy workers, this book is also a survival guide for anyone interested in exploring the many layered realms of spirit and energy while maintaining a healthy state of well-being. Think of these practices as spiritual first aid. The simple exercises within can be used not only for clearing the wreckage of past and present traumas associated with our physical day to day experiences but also those encountered during spirit work journeys. Delving into the realms of powerful spirits and their associated energies is often an exciting experience which can also create psychic debris, take a hit on our energetic reserves, and ultimately affect our health. In this book my hope is to provide some simple ways of becoming and also remaining healthy and whole.

Part of this book is about journeying toward wholeness by reclaiming the lost, fragmented, or compromised parts of your spirit. It is a guide to healing that which cannot be seen, but often permeates every room in the house of your life. I thought it was important to place *Real Book of Shadows* as the second book in the *Spirit Work Series* because it is vital for those of us who communicate and engage in spirit work to be (at least on most days) in a spiritually whole and healthy state.

The first part of this book introduces you to the energetic anatomy of spirit, and provides an overview of the chakra system and the layers of the aura. Next we cover basic methods of sensing energy and how to send or direct energy, as well as the use of Dream Walking. After this we examine the concept of negative psychic cords, what they are, how to dissolve them, and how to prevent them from reforming again. The last part of this book gets into the more complex matters of Shadow Work, Soul Retrieval, and Past Life Healing.

The types of energetic care, for self and others, described in this book are essential as a means for anyone who seeks energetic and spiritual wholeness. This is especially true if you decide to engage in the sort of spirit work practices where you are more likely to encounter negative entities, such as spiritual cleansing and protection, spirit rescue, spirit release, and exorcism. Your body, mind, and spirit will always fare better and be more effective if you are not struggling with the shadow aspects of self, negative psychic cording, fragmentation of the soul, past life intrusions, or any other energetic imbalance.

The intent of this book is to help you set up a safe and secure energetic foundation within your own energy base, or as a way of helping others to achieve the same, before moving forward into other aspects of spirit work. All of the practices described within can be used for you or they may be used as a way for guiding and helping another person to heal.

Becoming familiar with energy is the key to discernment in all aspects of spirit work and spirit communication. Working with energy patterns in the physical realm resonates in the nonphysical realms as well. As you become familiar with the energy emanating from the people around you in the earthly realm, you will have an easier time detecting or discerning the energy of spirit as the interpretation of these energies are similar in all realms. The positive energy of a person with good intentions will feel very similar to the energy of a positive spirit with good intentions. Alternately, that sick feeling that you get in the pit of your stomach when you are interacting with a negative person with bad intentions will also show up when you interact with a negative spirit who has bad intentions.

Also the changes you feel when perceiving something unhealthy in the physical realm (such as in a person, place, or object) will also translate over into what you perceived in the spirit realm. An example of this is when you run your hands over the aura of a person, place, or object and sense a notable difference in tactile sensations as a means of diagnosing an imbalance.

Another important aspect of working with energy is learning how to move it, as spirit is energy. Many forms of spirit work are about the movement of energy. In this book you are introduced to simple, safe and highly effective ways of sending and directing spiritual energy.

There are many spirit realms and spirit work often requires that we go to spirit rather than waiting to see if spirit will come to us. I believe most of you will see why this often wouldn't be very effective. How many times in the physical world have you waited for a letter, phone call, or a visit? When first starting out, one of the easiest ways to go to spirit is by bridging the physical and nonphysical realms via Dream Walking. The dream realm acts as a natural bridge which can easily be accessed and is a great starting off point to communicate with anyone, whether they are in the physical or nonphysical realm. Later in this book you will journey to the Pool of Memories to access the Akashic Records during Soul Retrieval

Shadows, unresolved issues, emotional baggage, negative psychic cords, and fragmentation of the soul due to past trauma or other causes, are the most common reasons which cause us to feel disconnected. Symptoms may be experienced as a mild separateness, or lack of connection, to others; both in the physical realm and the spirit realm. In more severe cases, we might also feel disconnected from ourselves. Some may referred to this as experiencing a dark night of the soul, while others describe feeling as if they have a "hole in the soul", and still others may say that they feel like a part of them is missing.

Shadows are created when people reject what they see as the undesirable parts of themselves. They may consciously or subconsciously hide, repress, or deny these aspects and push them down so far and for so long that they end up forming a shadow self. Many believe that the shadow is negative but this is not truly the whole story. The shadow self is actually made up of what the person believes is negative or unacceptable about the self, often combined with negative self dialogue, or rehashing the past and not being able to let go. The shadow itself may or may not actually be negative. Often it is the rejection of self on some level which is more damaging to the individual, rather than the shadow aspect itself. Shadows often reveal themselves when we consciously or subconsciously reject other people around us because they display the same characteristics which we reject in ourselves.

None of us will ever totally get rid of the shadow aspects of self but there is much power in seeing the shadow for what it is and understanding how the unwanted aspects of it formed. Being able to recognize and understand our own shadowy aspects goes a long way in becoming more whole and balanced. Just remember, shadow work is not done for the purpose of picking apart all the nasty or horrible little things about you, but it is about being honest with yourself.

I believe the material in this book will appeal to you dear reader, whether you are a new or experienced intuitive, psychic, medium, shaman, witch, magician, energy healer, root worker, paranormal investigator, or anyone else who wishes to maintain a healthy body, mind, and spirit in your day to day life, or while exploring the spirit realms. The language I use tends to be more spiritual rather than religious. It is my hope that I will be able to share experiences with anyone interested in this topic, whether you are Wiccan, Pagan, belong to a mainstream religion, or are just seeking spiritual wellness.

In the books that follow I cover a wide range practices related to what I think of and have come to term as "spirit work," such as dream work, ancestral healing, soul retrieval, spirit rescue, spirit release, spiritual cleansing, protection, and exorcism. Also covered are topics of spirit communication tools, how to create and use your own spirit work deck, and the use of stones, crystals, and herbs within the context of spirit work. The practices explored throughout this book series are derived from many diverse spiritual and energetic practices, such as energy healing, shamanism, root work, witchcraft, independent spiritualism, and a vast array of religio-magical practices from ancient mainstream religions, Paganism, Wicca, as well as my own experiences.

I have come to realize that our spirit is but a drop in the well of our souls and that our spirit's current trip through life is but a small part of the bigger journey of our soul. We each have the responsibility to care for the physical, mental, emotional, and spiritual aspects of ourselves throughout each journey. We need to have a common language to communicate about healing our energetic spiritual selves, just as doctors and nurses do to communicate about physical healing. On that note, let us next take a look at what makes up our energetic, spirit bodies and some of the common language used to describe it.

CHAPTER ONE
THE ENERGETIC ANATOMY OF SPIRIT

Many energy workers believe that often times, the last place that illness or disease manifests its appearance is in the physical body. The rationale for this is much of the time the imbalance that causes illness or disease begins in our mental, emotional, or spiritual bodies. Whenever that flow of life force which animates us all is disrupted, or blocked, by negative thoughts, emotions, and feelings, it creates an imbalance. If the imbalance is not corrected, the continued stress of the imbalance will resonate through to your physical body.

The reverse is also true; if you have a fractured bone, your physical body has a significant imbalance. If the imbalance is not corrected, the imbalance of your physical body may affect your mental, emotional, and spiritual wellbeing. The pain and stress may cloud and depress your thoughts, feelings and spirit.

Since I will be covering subjects having to do with the energy field surrounding us; this would be a good place to cover the basic anatomy of the Aura and the 7 Major Chakras.

Brief Overview of the 7 Major Chakras - and a few other ones:

The complete chakra system is a complex one that I would not be able to cover here. The information I give here is very basic and meant to be used as a launching off point. There are many wonderful books written on this subject. For those of you who would like to do further research, I have listed some excellent books to begin with, in the bibliography section.

What I will cover here is general information on the seven major chakras and the characteristics that they are most often associated with, and how this information can be applied to spirit work in regard to the healing of self and others.

It is interesting to note that there is sometimes conflicting information coming from different philosophies, resources, and books regarding chakra characteristics. You may find with some sources the colors of the chakras are different; you may also find differences with how the chakras spin. Some sources report that the chakras spin clockwise, others say counterclockwise, and yet others believe that the chakras alternate; with the 1st, 3rd, 5th, and 7th Chakras spinning in one direction, and the 2nd, 4th, and 6th Chakras spinning in another direction. Some resources relate that the 1st and 7th Chakras do not point front to back, but rather point up and down. You will find differences in how many Major, Secondary, and Minor Chakras there are. And, there is surprisingly, some sources which make no mention of the Back Chakras at all; or if they are mentioned, their importance is not stressed.

This conflicting information can be confusing, but do not let that put you off. The differences will not impact or change how you perform spirit or energy work.

The Seven Major Chakras

Chakras are the energy centers of spiritual power contained within the human body. The term chakra is a Sanskrit word that literally translates to spinning wheel or disc. In yoga, meditation, and Ayurveda, this term refers to the wheels of energy throughout the body. There are Seven Traditional Major Chakras which aligned the spine, starting from the base of the spine, through to the crown of the head. Chakras are visualized as swirling wheels of energy where matter and consciousness meet. There are also many minor or secondary Chakras in the body. Each major Chakra controls or manages our most vital functions, and works in alliance with each other, as well as with all the other secondary and minor Chakras.

Chakras are not physical but they are a part of your physical body. Most consider the size of a chakra to be approximately the size of your palm. Their spinning spiral forms a vortex with a space, or vacuum at the center of it, which draws in the Universal Life Force; a portion of each chakra extends out of the front and back of your body. That is why if any of your Chakras are blocked or corded, it can compromise both your physical and energetic fields.

The Root Chakra, aka Base Chakra, or *Muladhara* **(Sanskrit):** This Chakra is located at the base of the spine and is associated with survival. It represents our need for security, home, and all things related to the survival instinct. The Sanskrit term *Muladhara* translated means "root." The color Red is correlated to this Chakra.

The 2nd Chakra aka Sacral Chakra, Sexual Chakra, or *Svadhisthana* **(Snaskrit):** This Chakra is located above the pelvic area in the lower abdomen and is associated with sexuality. It represents passion, emotions, sexuality, creativity, and the creation of new life. The Sanskrit term *Svadhisthana* translated means "sacred home of the self." The color Orange is correlated to this Chakra.

The 3rd Chakra aka Solar Plexus Chakra, or *Manipura* (Sanskrit): This Chakra is located just below the sternum and represents personal power. It is the center of our vitality, energy, personal power, and motivation. It is also thought to be associated with clairsentience. The Sanskrit term *Manipura* translated means "inner sun" or "seat of the soul". The color Yellow is correlated to this Chakra.

The 4th Chakra aka Heart Chakra, or *Anahata* (Sansrit): This Chakra is located at the center of the chest; behind the heart and is associated with unconditional love. It represents compassion, love, and hope. The Sanskrit term *Anahata* translated means "unstruck or unbeaten". The colors Green and Pink are most frequently correlated to this Chakra.

The 5th Chakra aka Throat Chakra, or *Vishuddha* (Sanskrit): This Chakra is located in the throat area at the base of the larynx and represents communication. It is the center of our inner truth and the ability to express ourselves. The Sanskrit term *Vishuddha* translated means "purification." The color Blue is correlated to this Chakra.

The 6th Chakra aka 3rd Eye Chakra, or *Ajna* (Sanskrit): This Chakra is located in the center of the forehead; it is slightly above, and between, the eyebrows, and is associated with our intuition and psychic abilities. It is the center of our psychic perception having to do with clairvoyance. It is also thought to be in the area where our pineal gland is located.

The Sanskrit term *Ajna* translated means "perception." The color Indigo is correlated to this Chakra.

The 7th Chakra aka Crown Chakra, or *Sahasrara* (Sanskrit): This Chakra is located at the top of the head; specifically, at the "soft spot" on a newborn baby's head. This spot is thought to be where the soul enters the physical body at birth, and departs at time of death. The Crown Chakra represents our connection to the Divine and Universal Life Force. This is the center through which we receive Divine Love and Universal Energy. The Sanskrit term *Sahasrara* translated means "Crown." The three colors that are most frequently correlated to this Chakra are: White, Gold, and Violet.

Note: Understand that the 7 Major Chakras are portals to all the other Secondary or Minor Chakras because the whole Chakra System is interconnected.

In recent years we have seen the addition of other Chakras as the system of thought has been expanded upon by some energy workers who view the Major Chakra System as being made up of 13 energy centers rather than the 7 Traditional Major Chakras; and so they bear mentioning here and I will list them below. Some believe these 6 additional Chakras to be located outside of the body, unlike the 7 Traditional Major Chakras; while others believe that the chakras are both inside and outside of the body; and yet others believe that all 12 (really 13) are inside the body. Yikes! Talk about confusing!

The reason they bear mention here is because the concept of these additional Chakras contain the premise of our connection to the entire universe and our connection to the earth and sky energies, and to the entire array of dimensions. Hey, I love a good dimension builder. Some of you may have already jogged a sense of other energy centers, or portals as you've moved along in your development. Currently there exists a couple of different systems emerging for talking about the additional chakras; most of these systems appear to have the same additional chakras, but- the order in which they are presented is different. To keep things less confusing there will only be one list of these other Chakras below; just keep in mind that when doing further research, you may find these Chakras listed in a different order. Also I've noticed that most of these emerging systems of newer identified Chakras do not have specific colors correlated to them. The Traditional 7 Major Chakras follow the spectrum of the rainbow. Some of the systems of newer identified Chakras may add colors associated with metals, or other elements, such as; platinum, gold, So here they are listed below:

The 0th (Some say 8th or 10th) Chakra aka The Earth Chakra or Earth Star Chakra: I love to perceive this Chakra as the 0th Chakra; much like the Tarot's Fool; this

Chakra begins our journey through the rest of the Major Chakras discussed. This Chakra is located about one to three feet beneath your feet, and is the energy center that connects you to Mother Earth. It represents our connection to the planet, a connection to the feeling of oneness in nature, and of being in sync with your earthly journey through life. Spending time in nature, and grounding exercises help to keep this Chakra balanced. The colors Brown or Green are sometimes correlated to this Chakra.

The 8th (Some say 9th) Chakra aka The Soul Star Chakra: This Chakra is located about 6 inches about the head and the Crown Chakra. Some refer to this Chakra as the "seat of the Soul." It is
thought to be where our soul, containing all the information from previous lives, resides; and governs the energy of past lives and karmic memory. It is also considered to be the home of the "Higher Self." This is the Chakra of Astral Travel. When this Chakra is activated, it is thought to be possible to access the Akashic Records (all the information about the soul's journey), to have insights into past lives, and different dimensions. The colors Silver or White are sometimes correlated to this Chakra.

The 9th Chakra aka The Spirit Chakra: This Chakra is thought to be located about 12 to 18 inches above our heads and is associated with our spiritual connections to the higher realms, and communication with the Universe and higher vibrational beings; such as Spirit Guides, Angels, and other Light Spirits. This is the Chakra of intuition by direct revelation. When this Chakra is opened, you will be sure to experience recurrent synchronicities reinforcing the "knowing" or feeling that all in the Universe is connected by the flow of spirit. The energy of this Chakra supports the letting go of expectations, and feelings that trigger the need to control. Spirit will work for you and through you if you get out of the way of your *self* and allow yourself to be spirit led. If allowed and not blocked, Spirit will always lead you toward your highest purpose. Know that you will always get what you need (maybe not always what you want- as these are sometimes two different things), even when you don't know what *it* is. The color Gold or White is sometimes correlated to this Chakra.

The 10th Chakra aka The Universal Chakra: This Chakra is located above the 9th Chakra, or Spirit Chakra, and is associated with aligning ourselves with the Universal flow of energy. When this Chakra is activated, it opens us up to living life aligned with our Higher Selves. We have become one with the Universe as light beings and are more closely linked with Spirit Guides and Angels. The color mixtures of Violet, Gold, and Silver are sometimes thought to be associated with this Chakra.

The 11th Chakra aka The Galactic Chakra: This Chakra is thought to be located above the 10th Chakra, or Universal

Chakra, and is associated with the higher ascension of our souls. While it is thought to be possible for everyone to activate this Chakra, not many people reach this heightened level of spirituality. It is thought that when this Chakra is activated, things such as teleportation and instant manifestation are possible as time and space no longer have any meaning. Communication with the highest of Ascended Masters is possible and it is believed that you become a channel for enlightenment and healing on a planetary level. The color mixtures of Violet, Gold, and Silver are sometimes thought to be associated with this Chakra.

The 12th Chakra aka The Divine Gateway Chakra, sometimes called the God's Head Chakra: Yep, it's location is above the 11th Chakra, or Galactic Chakra. It's the top of the Chakra chain! This is believed to literally be the gateway, that once opened or activated, connects us to the Divine Source. With this Chakra activated, we become one with the Source, we are able to travel to other worlds and dimensions. We would become channels for peace and love, and become agents in bringing about spiritual ascension to the world. Pretty heady stuff! Who knows, if more people aim for opening up higher Chakras, perhaps the result would be a higher spiritual planetary shift. The colors sometimes correlated to this Chakra are said to be multi-faceted and multi-colored; one school of thought is possibly an iridescent Black, as Black is the culmination of all colors, others believe a golden-white, or a combination of colors that are sometimes referred to as "opalescence" or "iridescence." Another thought is one that supposes that a color beyond our perception would be correlated to this Chakra of the highest vibration.

You might be thinking- why no solid or agreed upon color associations with ethereal body Chakras 8 – 12? This extended system is most often seen to add colors associated with metals or other elements; such as silver, gold, and platinum; or color combinations that some refer to as "iridescence" or "opalescence" for the highest frequencies.

Other Chakras you may see referenced to, might include:

The Pineal Chakra: Some folks believe that this Chakra is located in front of, or on top of, the Pineal Gland; which is located behind your eyes in the very center of your brain. Other folks believe that this is the same as the 6th Chakra aka the 3rd Eye Chakra. This tiny gland is shaped like a pine cone and is the reason that it was named for it. This is the gland that secretes Melatonin which stimulates sleep, regulates our body clock, and controls our daily biological rhythms. This gland is believed to be the connecting link between the physical and spiritual worlds. When this Chakra is clear and activated it helps you to communicate with spirits and access hidden realms. It is believed to bridge the understanding to your inner self, or spiritual self, and is often activated by those entering the journey of a lightworker.

The Cerebellum Chakra: Some folks report that this Chakra is located at the back of your neck at the juncture of where the head and neck meet. (That is also the physical location of the Cerebellum.) While others report that this Chakra is actually located above the Crown Chakra and you will see it sometimes referred to by some sources as the 8th Chakra. This Chakra has been referred to as the "Well of Dreams" and inspires prophetic dreaming or "dreaming true." It is believed to be the next portal to Divine dimensions after the Crown Chakra and enables one to open up to the Divine Source. This center is also believed to enable the individual to achieve out-of-body, or Astral Projection; and also being a direct portal to the higher realms, it facilitates higher spiritual perception and wisdom. The color associated with this Chakra is Black.

The Thymus Chakra: This Chakra is thought to be located between the heart and the throat area, and is sometimes called the Higher Heart Chakra. Some also refer to this as the Gratitude Chakra because when activated this Chakra helps you to see the beauty and feel the gratitude wrapped into our day to day lives. It is also thought to bridge between the Traditional Heart Chakra and the Throat Chakra, connecting your heart energies to your words and facilitating communication with compassion.

The Sacred Heart Chakra: This Chakra is located just below the Heart Chakra and slightly to the left. This Chakra is believed to work together with the energy of our Heart Chakra to increase and expand our consciousness and feelings of unconditional love. It also develops the ability to receive messages from unseen worlds with increased intuitive feeling and clairsentience.

The Core Star Chakra: This Chakra is located above the Traditional 2nd Chakra aka Sacral Chakra, and is close to the diaphragm. The Core Star Chakra is associated with the pursuit of esoteric knowledge, understanding our role in the world, and discovering our Soul Purpose. This Chakra represents the "Study of the Soul."

It is a good idea to become familiar with the main chakras, what their characteristics are like when balanced, what their characteristics are like when not balanced, and what can be done to correct the imbalance.

I would like to note that at the time of this writing, despite the many variations of additional chakra configurations, the additional energy centers that are most commonly referenced to are the Earth or Earth Star Chakra- which I've listed above as the 0th Chakra; and the first two additional chakras above the Crown Chakra- the Soul Star Chakra -which I've listed as the 8th Chakra, and the Spirit Chakra- which I've listed as the 9th Chakra.

THE 7 LAYERS OF THE HUMAN AURA

The Human Aura is a subtle energy field surrounding the human body, created by molecules, atoms, and cells. The elements contained within this energetic field coexist and interact with each other, creating this subtle, magnetic, multidimensional field of energy. The word Aura is a Latin word translated to mean "Light" or "Glow of Light."

Many believe that the Aura that is part of your essence, and is a highly complex system that is not yet totally understood. Much of our core, individual information such as all of our thoughts, feelings, and our very consciousness, permeates with, and are stored in the Aura. It contains every one of our life experiences from the moment we are born.

Our physical, mental, emotional, and spiritual health is reflected in the Aura; the Aura is also the place where illness and disease often shows up before manifesting any symptoms in the physical body. It is important to note that the Chakras are one of the main sources of communication between the Aura and the physical body.

Another important aspect to remember is that all living things (and sometimes inanimate objects), such as plants, trees, and animals, have an Aura. Many are not as complex as the Human Aura but all operate in much the same way.

Basic Description of the Aura

Depending on your physical, mental, emotional, and spiritual health, your Aura may extend anywhere from four to six feet from the physical body. Often times, more spiritually developed individuals will have Auras that extend outward further than this. Many people who are able to "see" the Aura describe it as being egg-shaped; or describe it as the person being surrounded by a bubble of light that radiates out around them, it is sometimes seen consisting of shimmering colors.

The Layers or the Aura

Sometimes these layers are referred to as Subtle Bodies," Energy Bodies," "Auric Layers," or "Energy Fields." I like onion analogies, so I'll stick to the use of the term "layer" or "Auric Layer."
I tend to perceive the Human Aura as being composed of seven layers that surround the physical body. There are some sources that describe more layers, but most detail a variation

of the seven layers that I will describe here. The seven layers, listed in order from the innermost one that is closest to the physical body and moving out toward the outermost layer are named as follows: The Etheric Layer; The Emotional Layer; The Mental Layer; The Astral Layer; The Etheric Template Layer; The Celestial Layer; and The Ketheric Layer. Below I have listed a brief overview of each.

The Etheric Layer: The Etheric Layer is the first Auric Layer. The spiritual meaning of Ether is of the element of Spirit; it is thought to be the state formed between energy and matter. This layer lays closest to the body and extends approximately one to two inches away from it. It is sometimes described as being a blue or gray color depending on the health of the individual. This layer acts as an actual map for the physical body where illness or injury may first show up; and it contains all the physical impressions of the body's health or deficits; as we as all of the impressions of the individual Chakras, and the Chakra System's health and deficits. Blockages may be able to be detected by scanning.

The Emotional Layer: The Emotional Layer is the second Auric Layer; and it extends approximately two to five inches outward from the physical body. This layer contains the swirling energy of all of our ever-changing emotions. Blockages can occur here when unresolved emotions become stored within it. This layer is often perceived in a wide array of colors as they relate to the emotions contained there. Usually positive emotions emanate bright colors, while negative or unresolved emotions emanate dark colors.

The Mental Layer: The Mental Layer is the third Auric Layer, it extends outward approximately five to nine inches away from the physical body. This layer contains all our mental processes and will act as a reflection of the conscious mind. It stores all logic, thoughts, ideas, and beliefs. Ideas and inspiration are born and developed here. Mental health issues will also manifest and be reflected in this layer of the Aura. Those who can perceive the Aura describe this layer as a vibrant yellow which may become brighter or duller depending on the amount of energy being processed there.

The Astral Layer: The fourth Auric Layer is the Astral Layer, which extends approximately nine to thirteen inches outward from the physical body. It is the midpoint layer between the inner three Auric Layers, and the outer three Auric Layers. The Astral Layer serves as a portal, or a bridge between the physical realm and the spirit realm. This is an important layer in performing spirit work because each layer in the Aura affects the layer next to it. If you are having a hard time with some of your spirit work; you may have something going on within the first three layers of your Aura on a physical, emotional, or mental level. Clear and balance these first three levels and you may find your spirit work comes back on track. Many folks report seeing the colors of this level expressed as a rainbow bridge.

The Etheric Template Layer: The Etheric Template is the fifth Auric Layer and extends approximately one to two feet outward from the physical body. The primary purpose of this layer is to keep the first Auric Layer – The Etheric Layer, in place. It carries a template of the physical body on a higher spiritual level within this layer. Also found within this layer is your true inner identity, your current state of being, and all your possible futures on this physical plane. The color most commonly reported with this Auric Layer is a dark, cobalt blue.

The Celestial Layer: The sixth Auric Layer is The Celestial Layer. This layer extends about two to three feet outward from the physical body. This is the layer of feelings and emotions within the spiritual plane; it is the space of experiencing unconditional love and the gnosis of spiritual ecstasy. The Celestial Layer resonates the subconscious mind; it is a space of universal love and group consciousness. Those who are able to perceive the Celestial Layer describe it as a subtle but bright, soft-hued, shimmering light.

The Ketheric Layer: The seventh Auric Layer is the Ketheric Layer. This layer can extend outward approximately three to five feet outward from the body, depending on the individual's spiritual state; as it will expand as spirituality increases. The energies contained within it are of the highest frequencies of all the layers and is associated with the Divine or Universal Consciousness. Within it are what some refer to as your life plan, or soul contract and reflects all experiences and events that your soul has ever experienced. This layer is our spiritual template and is immortal; and while the other layers will dissipate with time; this is the only layer that will always exist, even after death. This layer is all knowing and is what becomes one with the Divine Source. Some believe that after death it will reincarnate in newly formed physical bodies, with the information accumulated from previous lives still contained within it; enabling this layer to be accessed for the Akashic records. Those that are able to see this Auric Layer describe it as a vibrant, rapidly pulsating, golden light.

CHAPTER TWO
WORKING WITH ENERGY

The Intersection of Energy, Spirit, & Magic

I have been a practitioner of shamanic witchcraft as well as a registered nurse for a long time (since the 80's) and I was initially attracted to studying Reiki as an adjunct to health care in my nursing practice. On my journey to becoming a Reiki Master-Teacher and working with the Universal Energy, I realized how interconnected magic, spirit work, and energy are. Before we get into some of the nuts and bolts of working with energy, let's define energy, spirit, magic, and the inner realms, and take a brief look at how they intersect and magnify each other.

Energy, as the term is used in this book, can be described as the flow and matrix of all life and matter. Reiki practitioners and other energy workers often term it as the "universal life force" or "universal energy." It is the core energy of creation which sustains the universe (and the extended multi-verse.) As we are all a part of this energy, it is always freely available to us. (Note: you do not need to be a Reiki practitioner to access this energy!) Many believe that this flow of energy is generated from a Divine Source or Mother/ Father God/ Goddess Source. Energy exists in a variety of forms which may often change but cannot truly be destroyed.

Energy can be influenced or worked with here in the physical realm, or it can be worked with in the nonphysical or inner realms. Whatever realm the energy is worked with, it will also affect or resonate in a similar way within the other realms. (Please note that I use the terms nonphysical realms and inner realms interchangeably.)

You might be wondering what exactly are the nonphysical or "inner realms," are they just your imagination? And what exactly is your imagination?

The *inner realms* are not make-believe and they do not reside within your mind, *but* they are accessed by your mind. Your imagination is the key to unlocking the inner realms, but the inner realms themselves are not imaginary. The inner realms are actually the nonphysical worlds outside of ourselves which some folks refer to as the astral plane.

One way to define imagination is the ability to generate a structure in your head. This structure can be creative, such as composing a song or a piece of art in your head but can also go way beyond these simple acts. Think of the imagination as a continuum. Visualize it as a keyboard. You might play one note over and over again or you might generate an entire opera. Many notes may be played on the keyboard of your imagination. Along with imagination, willingness and open-mindedness help to open the doorways of the inner realms. Later in this book, the journey of Soul Retrieval requires you to enter the inner realms, but I'm getting ahead of myself, for now let us just focus on a few definitions.

The term *spirit*, as it is used in this book, can be described as the vital essence or animating force within all living things. Many believe this definition to also extend to the spirit of places such as rivers, mountains, stars, and planets. Some may use the terms spirit and soul interchangeably but many believe that the soul is infinite and that each incarnation on earth is just a part of the soul known as *spirit* which makes up the total soul being.

The term *magic*, as it is used here, is the power of intention and can take many forms, such as: positive thinking, affirmations, prayer, ritual, spell casting by use of herbs, symbols, talismans, or by receiving help through the alliance of spirits. Examples of this can be such things as channeling the Universal Energy into a healing candle, crystal, or glass of water for one who is ill; petitioning of any helpful spirits known for magical healing, such as Archangel Raphael, Jesus, Obalata, Oxala, Brigid (the goddess or saint), and Dr. Jose Gregorio; whispering a healing prayer, psalm, or verse (such as Psalm 23) onto seven Job's Tears before putting them into a mojo bag and placing them under the pillow of the sick; casting a healing candle spell at the full moon by setting the intention for the symptoms of illness to diminish as the waning moon grows smaller along with the melting of the candle; or writing out a healing spiritual petition statement, much like a *himmelsbrief*, and placing it under a specially designated candle.

Many see the practice of magic as a way of collaborating with the universe to create change. This blend of your own will and Divine will is sometimes referred to as co-creating. Much like electricity, magic is a form of energy, it is neither good nor bad, and is dependent upon intention. Choose your intention carefully in all matters, as according to universal law, what you put out will return to you magnified many times over. Set the intention in all actions to be for the highest good of all.

Magic and spirit are both just different forms of energy and variations of the universal life force that flows through everyone and everything. The practices covered in this book might be seen by some as forms of working with energy, for others it is seen as working with spirit, and for still others it might be seen as a form of magic. I believe that the practices here encompass and magnify all three of these aspects and can be used for healing yourself or others in the physical or nonphysical realm.

The true intersection of energy, spirit, and magic starts with the core action of channeling universal energy. We are not using our own energy for most of the practices outlined in this book and the other books of this series. You can easily see why. If we were using only our own energy for these practices, we would quickly become depleted, destroy our immune system, and decimate our own health and vitality. When we set our intention for the universal energy to flow through us, we revitalize ourselves as much as we do those we are trying to help.

Another amazing aspect of inviting the flow of universal energy through us is that this flow of energy sets up a natural barrier of protection. Universal Energy is intelligent and will flow through us like a one-way street, there is no "back wash." What I mean by this is if you have set the intention for universal energy to flow through you while working with an unhealthy area of energy (yours or somebody else,) this sacred energy will flow through you and to the area where it is most needed, there is no backward flow, and in this way you are naturally protected from any unwanted energies entering your personal energetic space. For these reasons most of the exercises contained here start out with the channeling of universal energy. This simple act of channeling the Universal Energy allows you to become the intersection of energy, spirit, and magic.

Now let's begin by taking a look at some very simple and fundamental exercises for working within this intersection of energy, spirit, and a little magic!

Energy Scanning

Energy scanning can be done on any person, place or thing. In spirit work, energy scanning may be performed to detect energy imbalances, psychic energy cords, or spirit attachments. Energy Scanning can be done with your hands, with your eyes, or remotely by entering a visionary process.

Before You Begin:

Call on the Universal Energy to flow through you.
Ask your Spirit Guides and Allies to be near, in case you need their guidance or assistance.

Before you practice any of the exercises in this book, prepare yourself by Channeling the Universal Energy. This will ground and center you while providing built-in protection. Note that Channeling the Universal Energy was covered in Book One of the Spirit work Series but is listed below for your convenience. You may wish to record yourself and listen to it for future sessions.

Channeling the Universal Energy:

This exercise will ground and center you before drawing in the universal energy. You will feel energized and surrounded by protection.

Relax and take a number of slow, deep, full, cleansing breaths; in through the nose, and out through the mouth.

Set your intention to invite the Universal Energy to flow through you, cleansing and balancing each cell of your body; fortifying your mental and emotional well-being, and awakening and increasing your psychic vision and spiritual awareness, while strengthening your connection to the Divine Source.

Begin with grounding and relaxation.
Give your head, your heart, your body, and your soul permission to relax.
Breathe in and out.
(many find it helpful to count to 3 as you inhale, and 3 as you exhale)
Cast off all tension and all stress.

Begin with sensing waves of relaxation, washing down from the top of your head and gently flowing downward, all the way to your toes.

Feel these waves of light flowing downward, moving through you, cleansing and balancing each cell of your body.

Continue to breathe slow and deep, as these waves of relaxation flow
Down, down, down and down- out through the bottom of the soles of your feet. And down even further connecting you to the earth.

Visualize energy cords, extending downward from the bottom of your feet, and reaching deep, deep, deeper into the earth, clearing away any obstacles or unwanted energy, where it is transformed into clear, balanced, and usable energy.

Now sense this clear and balanced energy moving upward from the earth and traveling up through your feet and flowing upward, through your body in waves of healing, relaxing light, which renews your soul.

Feel these waves of light move upward from the soles of your feet and flowing upward to the top of your head; and continuing up, up, upward and out of the top of your head; exiting through the Crown Chakra, where it continues further and further upward, connecting you to the Source of Spirit.

You are now grounded and balanced. Allow your mind to remain quiet and receptive. Allow yourself to remain within this space of connection between the Earth's energies and the Cosmic energies.

Now ask the Universal Energy to flow in and through you.

See or sense the Universal Energy flowing downward from its Source as a dazzling, vibrant, golden white light, See it flowing downward, and entering the top of your head, through your Crown Chakra and flowing downward; Cleansing and fortifying your entire being.

See or sense this Universal Energy flowing downward moving through you; cleansing and balancing each chakra, healing and revitalizing each cell.

When this Energy reaches the Heart Chakra, see or sense the energy split three ways: continuing down your body and flowing down both arms, until you feel a fullness and tingling sensation in your hands and fingertips

The Energy continues to flow throughout your entire body, down your legs and into your feet, cleansing and balancing all energy within you.

Take a couple of deep, cleansing breaths; and open your eyes.

Take a few minutes to ground any excess energy, wriggle your fingers and toes, and perhaps get a drink of water.

You have now become a channel for Universal Energy. When first starting out, you may want to record the "script" above and listen to it. If you are able to, do it every day at first. The more you practice channeling the universal energy, the faster and more powerful it will flow. You will see in the following sections how this energy is incorporated or used in spirit work. You will be able to invite the Universal Energy to flow through you at any time by simply asking it to and then visualizing this stream of energy flowing downward and entering the top of your head through the Crown Chakra. I like to place my hands, palms down, on top of my thighs and silently state "energy on" or "energy flow," and this is enough to begin the stream of sacred energy through me.

Energy Scanning by Using Your Hands:

On a person, a healthy aura usually radiates outward a good 18 to 24 inches or more. An unhealthy or diminished aura may only radiate out 3 to 6 inches. Start out with your hands about 2 to 3 feet away and move in closer; stop when you feel heat, tingling, or pressure- you are now feeling the outer aura. Using your hands systematically move across the outer aura of the person, animal, object, or place.

To do this:

1) Briskly rub your hands together for 30 seconds to sensitize them.

2) Run your hands, with palms facing who or what you are scanning, in a systematic way (top to bottom, left side/ right side, etc.), over the exterior aura of the person, place, or thing.

3) Start out with your hands about 2 to 3 feet away. When you find the outer aura, note where it is and then move in to the inner aura, which is usually 4 to 6 inches from the body. Some folks like to start with their hands above the Crown Chakra and slowly move down over the Major Chakras. Make a sweep down the front and then make a sweep down the back.

4) Concentrate on the center of your palms as you do this.

5) Stop, or pause and make note, if you sense or feel any temperature changes- heat or cold spot; a tingling sensation; density; or sense energetic resistance, pressure, or presence.

Using Your Eyes:

As you advance; or if you are naturally very visual, you may begin to scan energy with your eyes by reading the aura. If you are just starting out try the Aura Gazing exercise below and build from there.

Aura Gazing

One great way to start out practicing aura gazing is to set up a white taper candle against a white wall. If none of your walls are white you might want to drape a white sheet in the background.

Get comfortable and free of distractions.

Light the candle.

Gaze at the candle flame and observe the shimmer or glow that surrounds the flame.

Allow your eyes to go into a soft focus. Sometimes it may be easier to see the aura when your eyes are slightly out of focus.

Now try to see or sense a similar but a more subtle shimmer around the entire candle, top to bottom and side to side.

It may be faint, and if you focus on it too intently, it may disappear.

After you are confident with this shimmer, begin to look for a similar, soft shimmer around other things like plants, animals, or people against a white background.

You might not see any colors at first; possibly only a glimmering sphere of light surrounding your subject.

As you advance, try to detect any gaps, dips, or protrusion, in the outline of the aura (or shimmer), and note what color it is. Is it the same color all around? Or are there several different colors depending on where you look? Don't concentrate too hard; usually the first color that you sense or see is the correct color.

Beaming Energy

Channeling, sending or "beaming" the Universal Energy may be done with your hands, eyes, or by using crystals or other objects that have been programmed to do this. Any of these methods can be used as a way to send extra energy to an area where it may be needed.

If you haven't already, before you practice beaming energy, call on the Universal Energy to flow through you. This will ground and center you while providing built-in protection.

When beaming Universal Energy to another person simply visualize rays of golden-white light which now flows through you, being channeled to the other person; either by using your hands, or your eyes. Allow the stream of energy to keep going until the target of the energy seems "full" or until you have a sense of being finished. Follow up afterwards by grounding any excess energy. Grounding can be quickly and simply done by visualizing all excess or unwanted energy flowing downward through your body and exiting out through the bottom of the soles of your feet, into the earth where it can be transformed. Then see this cleansed and renewed energy flowing back upward through the bottom of your feet and up through your body making you feel balanced and revitalized.

If you are using a crystal, use it in the same way after you have "programmed" it for the purpose of beaming energy. Do this by filling the crystal with energy sometime before you intend to use it. This can be done by holding the crystal in your hands, focusing on your intent, and asking the Universal Energy to flow through you and out through your palm chakras into the crystal.

Raising and Sensing Spiritual Energy

Practicing raising and sensing energy is a good exercise to use in not only sensing but also being able to physically feel spiritual energy. In this exercise you experience a combination of Divine Universal Energy and your own energy that will flow into your hands from your Solar Plexus Chakra (located about 2 inches above the belly button), by calling on the Universal Energy to flow through you.

Some folks report that the feeling of holding energy in their hands during this exercise is similar to a weak, magnetic repulsion. This is the same type of feeling you get when taking the two positive ends of two different magnets and try to put them together; the two fields of energy offer resistance; there is a feeling of pushing away. Other folks report a variety of sensations experienced; like an electrical feeling in the air; a shift in temperature; or a tingling, "pins and needles" sensation in the palms of your hands. Any of these are okay; we all experience this exercise differently.

Once you are able to sense this energy, you have gained a fundamental building block for spirit work and for healing self and others.

If you haven't already, call upon the Universal Energy. See this energy flow through you and around you.

Next:
Relax and breathe deeply.
Take in 3 deep cleansing breaths.
As you inhale, breathe in the golden-white light of Divine energy.
As you exhale, breathe out the gray mist of any anger, tension, or negativity, and let it go.

Know that any and all negativity is gone.
Begin to focus on the area of your Solar Plexus.
Feel a building of energy in the center of your being. (Solar Plexus)

Briskly rub your hands together for about 30 seconds.
Now hold your hands in front of you, about three feet apart, with the palms facing each other as you sense all of the positive energy that you have built up in your Solar Plexus flow into your hands.

As you exhale, blow into the area of the center space being held between your hands with the knowledge and intention of your energy combining with Divine Energy.

Relax. Become aware of any new information that you receive from your hands.
Do not try to analyze or create the experience. Allow it to happen naturally.

Slowly bring your hands together.
Notice any sensations.
Be aware of any feelings that come in layers or waves of very slight resistance; as these are the layers of your personal aura or energy body.

When you are done, wash your hands to remove any excess energy picked up during this exercise.

Sending or Directing Spiritual Energy

Start as you did before in the previous exercise for Raising and Sensing Spiritual Energy. Hold your hands about 3 feet apart with your palms facing each other. Slowly bring your hands together. Observe and notice any sensations.

When you hands are about 6 inches apart, imagine, sense, or visualize that you are holding a ball or a sphere of energy about the size of a baseball. At first this ball will just be an empty shell, but you are filling it with the energy between your hands. Some folks may see this energy in varying colors and forms such as; light, fire, or water. Through visualization you may make this ball of energy into any shape. You can stretch it out like taffy, or compress it down to the size of a pea.

Once you have a solid ball of energy floating between your hands, you can literally shape it to any form, and fill it with any intention. Have a very clear intention in your mind. You may want to make a silent statement of intent at this time. The point is to make sure that your message is very clear.

Psychic spheres can be programmed to do just about anything. Some of the common ways these spheres can be used are: to send blessings, to send healing energy, or even for getting somebody to call you. Distance is not a factor; this ball of energy can travel great distances to deliver your intentions.

After you have given this psychic sphere a shape, and filled it with your intention, release it. It should carry out your intentions as soon as you let it go. If you just made this sphere for practice, it should just naturally dissipate.

CHAPTER THREE
DREAM WALKING

Some people may call this dream visitation, dream journeying, or dream walking. Like distant mental influence, dream walking is another form of visioning or journeying; it is a way to visit another person while they dream. Within the energetic patterns surrounding us, dream walking is most often used as a way to link with the living but can also be used as a way to link to the dead. The dream realm serves as a natural bridge between all of us, whether living or dead.

We are all at our most vulnerable and also our most open and receptive while we sleep. Dream walking is one way to communicate something to the dreamer while they sleep. The dream walker may also be able to manipulate the environment and the events occurring within the dream world.

Never attempt dream walking with negative intentions toward the target (person) of your work. The spirit world operates in similar ways to the physical world. Like does definitely attract like. In the same way a person radiating joyful, positive energy attracts more of the same, so does the person with malevolent and evil intention. Walking into the spirit realms or dream realm with negative intentions will draw lower lying entities to you like flies to human waste. Hope is contagious but so is fear. Make your journey into dream walking with a clear mind and heart and you will be amazed at the results! Dream walking can be a useful tool for sending information, solving problems, and discovering answers.

Most people use dream walking as a way to contact the living but it can also be used to as a way to send healing or loving energy to one who is ill or lost, and it can also be used as a way of contacting the dead.

How to Contact the Living via Dream Walking

Be clear about your intention.

Know ahead of time what you want to communicate or find out.

Select a time you believe that the dream target will be asleep. Write out your dream target's name on a piece of paper; or have a photo of them handy.

I like to light one small, white candle to focus on initially.

To strengthen your intent you might optionally write the person's name on a piece of paper and place their name under the candle. Some people like to use a photo of the person or another personal item belonging to them. This is a nice touch but might not be necessary; use what works best for you.

Before I begin I will briefly channel the Universal Energy and ask my guides, allies, or ancestors for guidance and protection.

Visualize a protective shield surrounding you.

Focus on your intention and on the target of your dream walking and set your intention to link to their spirit.

Gaze into the candle flame as you breathe deeply and slowly.

Get into a relaxed state and allow your eyes to close.

As the door in your mind's eye opens- see yourself (or your spirit self) drawn upward with a gentle pull and then floating up and out of your body.

See yourself going up, up, upward. See yourself float through the roof of your house and moving through the air to where the person you seek to dream walk is located.

If you do not know where the person is located ask your spirit guide to lead you to the target (person).

See yourself float downward and into the room of the sleeping person.

Go next to them and see the energetic link between yourself and the other person. Many people see it as a vibrant bridge of energy extending from their heart or mind to the other person's heart or mind.

Allow yourself to stay there moving through their dreams. Notice any sensations or information coming to you while there. If your intention was to communicate something to this person, tell them now. If you were seeking an answer, ask your questions. If you want the person to contact you, tell them that they will do so upon waking in the morning.

If the purpose of this dream walk is to send love or healing energy visualize the person being surrounded with this loving or healing energy as you ask right then and there for the Universal Energy to flow through you. See yourself channeling this sacred energy into and through the other person. Continue to channel this energy until the other person feels "full" or until you feel that you are done. Talk to the person that you are sending healing energy to, tell them that they are filled with vibrant healing light and will wake up feeling refreshed and energized.

When it is done, say goodbye, see the energetic link between you and the other person dissolve, and then begin to journey back into yourself.

See yourself rising and floating back, through the night sky until you reach your home where you will descend back down into your body.

In your mind's eye, close the door that you went through to begin your dream walk.

Take a couple cleansing breaths. Wiggle your fingers and toes. Allow yourself to become aware of your surroundings.

When you feel ready, open your eyes.

Blow out the candle.

You may want to write down anything that you experienced, because just like dreams, a dream walk can be difficult to remember later on.

If you have another person that you trust highly, and they are agreeable, you may want to try practicing dream walking with each other. You may both end up pleasantly surprised at how effective it is.

CHAPTER FOUR
DREAM WORK

HOW TO CONTACT SPIRIT VIA DREAMS

We all dream. While in the dream realm the division separating our well of psychic power and the waking, analytical world grows thin or completely dissolves. Dreaming is not truly a passive or receptive state; it is the active essence of our soul erupting from our very core while spontaneously creating inter-dimensional connections. Many of our dreams carry messages, omens, and other sorts of information as a means of guidance, often from protective deceased loved ones, ancestors, or other guardian spirits. Dreams are where we can receive answers to our questions, connect with departed loved ones, find connections to past lives, or view visions of the future.

Although we may not remember, or may have spates of time where imbalanced sleep patterns or medication interfere, most people have an average of four to six dreams nightly. The act of dreaming recharges our intuitive/ psychic batteries, as well as fortifying our physical health.

Many ancient magical and spiritual traditions relate the belief that each of us have many souls or spirit selves, and that each of us has a dream spirit. Our dream spirit is able to journey to other realms, interact with other spirits, gather information, seek out answers, and go on magical adventures. While our body is awake, our dream spirit sleeps and the sleep/ wake cycle fortifies both our spiritual and physical bodies.

The dream realm serves as a bridge between worlds and is the most common means of receiving communication from other spiritual entities. Spirits of the dead can communicate with us via dreams, as can angels, saints, spirit guides, power animals, ancestors, master teachers, and other entities.

Dreams are a key to the fluid, magical realms of spirit and are often a catalyst to your own power. Through focus and intention we are able to enhance and use our dream state to receive guidance and answers, help and healing, and to connect with specific spirits. All dreams are significant but the ones to really pay attention to are: the last dream you have just before waking and the dream that another person has about you.

There are a couple of different ways to contact spirit and receive a dream visitation or message. Intention is the key. Maybe you seek dream contact to spend time with a departed loved one to be assured that they are okay, or perhaps you're seeking guidance or answers to a specific problem, so then your intent would be to receive a dream message from spirit to help answer your concerns. You might set your intention to be guided in your journey to spirit, or your intention might be that spirit come visit you, or you may set your intention that spirit simply provide a message. Many of the practices contained here can also aid the reception of prophetic dreams, and/ or dreaming true.

First, let's look at a few general guidelines. When initiating contact with spirit via dreams, always have a specific intention with a specific spirit in mind. Do not send out a general invitation to spirit, this would be like throwing the door open and inviting strangers into your personal space, and there's no way to tell who will show up. Another aspect to consider is whether to petition a spirit directly or indirectly by using a dream gateway guardian. There are many dream gateway guardians to be explored but for many of us a trusted spirit guide may serve as a gateway guardian.

I will go over a few different methods of inviting spirit into your dreams by using the power of intention in combination with one or more of the elements of earth, air, fire, or water to symbolize and amplify your intent. Any of the practices listed below can be effective and can be thought of as creating a powerful transmitter to draw a specific spirit to you in the dream realm, enable your dream spirit self to journey to the one you seek, or to receive answers, information, or guidance via symbols, dream scenarios, or by direct spirit to spirit interaction.

CHARGING YOUR MATERIALS

Spirit work can often involve utilizing various materials used as tools to enhance and power up your intent. These tools are usually natural items received from the earth, involving the elements of earth, air, fire, and water. Combining your energy, focus, and intent with the elements is the fuel of magic!

Magical energy lies quietly within everything waiting to be unlocked. And just how do we unlock this power? We unlock the power by sending/ channeling the flow of universal energy and our intention into the material we are using to power up our work.

There are many different ways to charge your materials. You might hold the item in your hands while focusing on your intention and ask the universal energy to flow through you and your hands, into the item you are holding. You might do the same action by using your eyes instead of your hands, or by inviting the universal energy to flow through your breath, while you recite your intention and visualize in your mind's eye the outcome of your desired goal.

Simple Charging Technique:

Hold the item sandwiched between both of your hands.

Take a couple of deep, cleansing breaths and clear your mind.

Bring the desired outcome you seek into your mind's eye.

Invite the universal energy to flow through you; you might trigger this by stating "energy flow."

Visualize this combination of your intention (desired outcome) and the universal energy flowing through you and out of your hands, into the object you are holding.

Stay with this energy flow until you begin to feel that you are "done" or that the object is "full."

Set your charged item to the side and withdraw your focus. Take a moment to ground your energy. Sometimes I'll shake my hands or stomp my feet to help reset my focus.

I usually like to end with saying thank you to the universal energy and the charged object.

DREAM CONTACT VIA THE ELEMENT OF EARTH

To contact the spirit of a deceased loved one, or an ancestor, you might write their full name on a piece of paper, or write out a spiritual petition, which is basically like writing a letter to them which includes your thoughts and intentions. This paper can be placed in a dream pillow or a dream mojo bag, which has been filled with spirit drawing and/ or dream enhancing herbs, and then placed under your pillow. The energy and focus that you put into the creation of a dream pillow, or dream mojo, also helps to solidify your intention, which plays a significant role in dream work.

Using the element of earth, some of the most powerful and traditional herbs used to incorporate in a dream pillow or mojo bag for spirit drawing are listed below.

BOTANICALS:

Acacia: since ancient times has been used to enhance personal psychic power and communicate with the dead.

Althaea Leaves or Root: reputed to draw benevolent spirits to you.

Angelica Root: aka as Holy Ghost Root, this root has a long time reputation for drawing higher vibrational spirits and is spiritually protective, especially of women and children.

Anise Seed & Star Anise: both of these botanicals boost psychic receptivity, dream work and dream recall.

Bay Leaves: has been used for spirit communication since ancient times. Combine Bay Leaf with Anise and Calendula for an especially powerful aid to dream work; is said to induce prophetic dreams and to promote the reception of insight and bring about answers by dreaming true.

Calendula: this brightly colored, golden flower is said to be useful in bringing about prophetic dreams aka dreaming true. Place Calendula under your pillow when seeking answers or guidance from the spirit realm.

Dittany of Crete: considered one of the most powerful herbs for manifesting spirits and as an enhancement to Astral Travel and dream recall.

Jasmine Flower: long known for its seductive and intoxicating fragrance, Jasmine also has a reputation for opening doorways in the subconscious and fostering vivid dream imagery.

Marjoram: in spirit work Marjoram is well known for its specialized and unique quality of lightening and brightening the mood of melancholy or angry spirits.

Mugwort: this herb is highly esteemed in metaphysical communities for the qualities of psychic and spirit communication enhancement. In years past, dream pillows were a common item sold in magical supply shops and Mugwort was always one of the main ingredients. Many old-time root-workers that are also psychic readers will carry a mojo or charm bag filled with Mugwort as they carry out their work.

Rosemary: this herb is used for remembrance of the dead. Use this herb when seeking contact with the dearly departed.

Vervain: aka Verbena, this herb is also known as the "Enchanters Herb." This is the main botanical long used by spirit workers for summoning "melancholy" spirits, such as those who died filled with grief, murder victims, spirits who died in accidents, or for those that possibly do not know or are in denial that they are dead. Vervain has the effect of lightening the vibration of many spirits of the dead.

Wormwood: aka Absinthe, Madderwort, Old Woman, and Crown for a King. Wormwood has an ancient, infamous reputation as the most powerful herbs used in calling, or summoning spirits of the dead.

Yarrow: another botanical used since ancient times. It is said that placing a packet of Yarrow beneath your pillow will bring about prophetic dreams. Use Yarrow in combination with Jasmine and Mugwort to receive messages and answers from spirit in the dream realms.

Both Dream Pillows and Mojo/ Charm Bags are like a spell within a bag, carrying your intention and fueled by correlating power objects. Listed below are some simple ways you can create these items for yourself.

HOW TO CREATE A DREAM PILLOW

Cut two pieces of fabric into same-sized squares and sew them together on three sides. (I usually make small ones, approximately 4 x 6 inches.)

Gather your botanicals. Make sure all herbs are completely dried.

Hold the botanicals in your hands and charge them with universal energy and your intention. Call upon your Higher Power, spirit guides, or any other spirits that you work with, or seek to work with and ask that they aid your work.

Ingredients that might produce hard edges or poke through the fabric (such as Bay Leaf or Yarrow) should be ground up.

Write out your name paper, prayer, intention, or spiritual petition.

If you like, lightly dress/ anoint the corners of the paper, herbal materials, and/ or corners of the cloth with an essential oil or a condition oil which correlates to your intent (such as Sandalwood Oil, or Frankincense Oil.) Note that a formulary and much more information on the creation of condition oils used in spirit work will be covered in the upcoming books of the Spirit Work Series.)

From the open end, fill the bag with the herbs and place the paper you have written out into the center of the bag while focusing on your intention.

Sew the open end of the bag up.

Place the dream pillow on or under your regular pillow so that you are directly or indirectly in contact with it while you sleep.

HOW TO CREATE A SIMPLE MOJO OR CHARM BAG

Creating a Mojo or Charm bag is very similar to creating a dream pillow.

Gather the cloth or bag that you will use. Many people like to use the little red flannel bags but you can use just about anything. I've used old hankies, babushka scarves, and scraps of cloth left over from other sewing projects. I like to take an approximately 9 x 9 inch square piece of cloth and cut off the four corners, making it into a circle.

If using a piece of cloth, you will need a length of string to tie it shut. I like to use natural hemp cord or jute, but any type of string will do.

Gather your botanicals. Make sure all herbs are completely dried.

Hold the botanicals in your hands and charge them with universal energy and your intention. Call upon your Higher Power, spirit guides, or any other spirits that you work with, or seek to work with and ask that they aid your work.

Write out your name paper, prayer, intention, or spiritual petition.

If you like, lightly dress/ anoint the corners of the paper, herbal materials, and/ or corners of the cloth with an essential oil or a condition oil which correlates to your intent (such as Sandalwood Oil, or Frankincense Oil.) Note that a formulary and much more information on the creation of condition oils used in spirit work will be covered in the upcoming books of the Spirit Work Series.)

Place the botanicals and the paper you have written out into the the bag while focusing on your intention. (I will sometimes wrap the paper around the botanicals so that they are surrounded with my intention, and then place it in the bag or cloth.)

Before "cinching" or tying the bag shut, "breathe it into life." Do this by holding the open end near your mouth, you may simply breathe into it, or recite an incantation, a prayer, or a statement of intent while purposefully allowing the breath of your words to enter the bag. Then quickly cinch or tie the bag securely shut.

Place the bag you have created under your pillow before sleep.

Note: do not allow anyone else to touch or open the bag, as it is believed that this will cause it to be robbed of the power contained within.

STONES & CRYSTALS

Another way to power up the focus of your dream work using the earth element is via the use of stones or crystals. Begin by carefully choosing a selected crystal that you will hold between your hands and charge it with universal energy. See, sense, or feel the universal flowing through you and out of your hands, into the crystal. Continue to do this until the crystal feels warm and "full" or until you feel it is done. (Cleanse the crystal prior to charging it either by rinsing with cool water or smudging it in the smoke of Sage or Frankincense and Myrrh.) Place the charged crystal by your bedside. Below are listed some of stones and crystals used in dream work.

CREATE A LINK TO SPIRIT GUIDES & GUARDIANS: Amber, Amethyst, Celestite, Labradorite, Moonstone, Clear Quartz, Rose Quartz, Selenite, Seraphanite, or Black Calcite.

ENHANCE DREAM RECALL: Amethyst, Celestite, Kyanite, Lapis Lazuli, or Moonstone.

FOR DREAM WALKING: Angelite, Carnelian, Celestite, Lapis Lazuli, Labradorite, Moonstone, Moqui Marbles, or Preseli Bluestone.

FOR SPIRIT JOURNEYING & ASTRAL TRAVEL: Amethyst, Apache Tear, Black Calcite, Black Tourmaline,

Carnelian, Celestite, Indigo Gabbro, Kyanite, Labradorite, Lapis Lazuli, Smokey Quartz, or Spirit Quartz.

DREAM CONTACT VIA THE ELEMENT OF AIR

Since ancient times there has been a belief in the magical qualities of botanicals. According to the Doctrine of Signatures, and even more ancient beliefs, it is thought that each plant carries with it a magical signature bestowed upon it by the Divine as to its true purpose, and provides the basis of magical herb lore. The practice of burning incense is believed by many to release the power of these botanicals, which has been combined with your intentions, so when the smoke of the incense rises, it carries your "message" to where (or who) it was intended to go to. Burning an incense of botanicals which carries the signature correlated to your intentions prior to going to sleep, is another powerful way to facilitate spirit contact via dreams.

Using the element of air (along with earth and fire) here are some of the most powerful and traditional single and combination botanicals used for spirit dream work:

SINGLE BOTANICAL INCENSE:

Copal: this aromatic tree resin is considered sacred incense in Mexico. Copal enhances dream states and attracts benevolent spirits.

Frankincense: used as incense, this aromatic tree resin has been highly valued since ancient times for attracting benevolent spirits while simultaneously repelling malevolent spirits.

Myrrh: this resin is known for its strong and somewhat intoxicating fragrance. Myrrh is extremely powerful, and when burned as incense, it will draw spirits like crazy! DO NOT burn it alone as a solo ingredient. It is best used in conjunction with other botanicals that are reputed to draw _benevolent_ spirits. That is why you will so often see Myrrh combined with Frankincense. To create powerful incense formula to burn in your bedroom before going to sleep, combine Myrrh, Frankincense, and Sandalwood in equal parts.

Sandalwood: highly valued as sacred and holy incense since ancient times. Although considered not quite as strong as Frankincense, Sandalwood also attracts benevolent spirits while simultaneously repelling malevolent ones; one of its perks is it also encourages relaxation and increased receptivity to spirit contact via dreams. Burn a bit of Sandalwood either alone, or in combination with

Frankincense and Myrrh, in your room before going to sleep for the night to facilitate dream contact with spirit.

INCENSE BOTANICAL COMBINATIONS:

To create one of the formulas listed below, I recommend that you first create a self lighting incense base and then add the ground up botanicals and/ or essential oils to it. With self-lighting incense, there is no need to use charcoal.

Self Lighting Incense Base
1 part very fine, untreated (no chemicals!) sawdust. (I prefer Maple or Pine)
1/3 part Yellow Sandalwood Powder
1 to 2 tsp of Salt Peter (Per cup of Self-Lighting Incense Base- adjust proportion as needed.)
Blend well

Then Add:

2/3 part of your chosen finely ground and powdered herbs and or resins
Blend well.

Then Add:

1 dropper (per cup) of either a correlated single essential oil, or a correlated combination of essential oils

Note: I like to make my incense blends powdery but with a slightly moist texture. This makes it easy to simply grab a pinch of it with my fingers and place a cone-shaped deposit of incense onto my censer, ready to light.

Important: Always use caution with Salt Peter as it is combustible around open flame.

Dream Walking Incense
Incense Base
Add Ground Herbs: Jasmine & Dittany of Crete
Add Essential Oils: Sandalwood
Blend well.

Dream Spirit Drawing Incense
Incense Base
Add Ground Herbs: Calendula, Mugwort, & Wormwood
Add Essential Oils: Sandalwood Oil alone or equal parts of Sandalwood, Frankincense, and Myrrh Oils.
Blend well.

Astral Dream Journey Incense
Incense Base
Add Ground Herbs: Anise, Dittany of Crete, Jasmine & Mugwort
Add Essential Oils: Sandalwood and/ or Ylang Ylang, and just a drop or two of Anise.

Blend well.

High Spirit Incense (simple version)
Incense Base
Add Ground Herbs: Athaea, Anise, Bay Leaf, & Wormwood
Add Essential Oils: Frankincense, Myrrh, & Bay
Blend well.

Spirit Guide Incense
Incense Base
Add Ground Herbs: Acacia, Angelica Root & Bay Leaf
Add Essential Oils: Copal
Blend well.

Drawing the Dearly Departed Incense
Incense Base
Add Ground Herbs: Rosemary, Mugwort, Wormwood (optional: Marjoram & Vervain)
Add Essential Oils: Sandalwood
Blend well.

Dream Message Incense
Incense Base
Add Ground Herbs: Yarrow, Jasmine, & Mugwort
Add Essential Oils: Sandalwood (Optional: a few drops of Ylang Ylang and 3 drops of Anise)
Blend well.

Note: anytime you suspect that the spirit you are seeking dream contact with may be caught up in issues of sadness or anger, add ground Marjoram or Vervain liberally to the incense you are creating, as these two botanicals are reputed to lighten the mood of spirit.

DREAM CONTACT VIA THE ELEMENT OF FIRE

Another way to send a powerful invitation to spirit (via the element of fire) is to charge a white candle which you have personalized to the spirit you wish to contact. Do this by carving the name, and/ or anything else that represents the spirit onto the candle, such as their date of birth, symbol, or sigil. Hold the candle in your hands, clear your mind, and channel the universal energy into the candle while focusing on your intent. See, sense or feel the universal flowing through you and out of your hands, into the candle. Continue to do this until the candle feels warm and "full" or until you feel it is done. Dress the candle by anointing it with an essential oil that attracts benevolent spirits such as Frankincense, Sandalwood, or a good quality Olive Oil. On a small piece of paper, write your spiritual petition (your intention, a prayer, or incantation) and place it under the candle. Light the candle while focusing on your intention. Allow the candle to burn for a select amount of time (usually 30 to 60 minutes) as you focus on the intent and then snuff it out. Do this near bedtime for best results and always practice fire safety, don't fall asleep while the candle is burning or leave it unattended. Repeat the act of lighting the candle, focusing on your intent and the spirit you are seeking contact with, and allowing it to burn for the allotted period of time before snuffing it out. Do this nightly until you receive your dream visitation.

DREAM CONTACT VIA THE ELEMENT OF WATER

I have saved the most powerful, yet the most simple for last. Water is associated with the deep well of human emotion and is known as the element of intuition, psychic power, and dreams. Spirits are attracted to water. It's no surprise that one of the most powerful ways to facilitate spirit visitation via dreams is to set out a glass of water which you have charged with universal energy in the spirit's name. Place the water at your bedside table before going to sleep (always dispose of it when you wake in the morning by pouring it into the ground or your garden.)

For any of these activities, also keep a notepad and pen next to the bed so that you are able to write down any dream activity, visitations, or messages received upon waking. Do the journaling as soon as possible as dreams have a way of fading from memory the longer we are awake. Read what you have written later on to interpret the information received.

Sometimes spirit will get the message right away and show up the very first night. Other times you may have to petition the spirit every night until they appear in your dreams.

CHAPTER FIVE
CLEARING PSYCHIC DEBRIS

PSYCHIC DEBRIS

Everyone is prone to accumulating psychic debris within the aura. Psychic debris can include anything from being exposed to anger, depression, negative energy patterns, particles or fragments of thoughts, intense feelings, the lower vibrations of others, close contact with lower vibration entities, any or all dark, heavy energy that can mess with your energy and weaken your aura. Shielding helps, but doesn't always suffice! For anybody involved in doing spirit work, and especially for those of us who tend to be empathic, it is essential to routinely clear your energy. It's important to do the quick Cleanse and Clear Routine on a daily basis, and you may also want to sometimes incorporate doing a Spiritual Cleansing Bath; especially after heavy spirit work, whenever feeling unbalanced or ungrounded, or anytime you suspect you might be accumulating psychic debris.

METHODS OF CLEARING PSYCHIC DEBRIS FROM PERSONAL ENERGY FIELDS

QUICK CLEANSE & CLEAR:

Cleanse and clear is really the same process of grounding and centering that we use prior to Channeling the Universal Energy. It is basically envisioning a cleansing and clearing light energy moving through you, top to bottom as you visualize cords of energy exiting the bottom of your feet and running deep into the ground.

The intent and process are the same but it is done in a more rapid and powerful manner. I do the Cleanse and Clear with focused intent by visualizing a powerful, cleansing light and seeing it *whoosh* through the center of my being, drawing everything into alignment as it also grounds any excess or unwanted energy, exiting through the cords at the bottom of my feet, grounding and transforming unwanted energy. At the same time this powerful cleansing light surrounds me and energizes me.

One way to do this:

Hold your hands above your head with your palms facing you. As you visualize the cleansing light flowing downward through you, and around you, quickly bring your hands downward in front of you and push outward at the bottom of your reach. Envision any potential thought forms, attachments, or any other unwanted forms of energy flowing downward and exiting out through the bottom of your feet and into the earth. While doing this you might verbalize a strong affirmation such as: *I now cleanse and clear.*

SPIRITUAL CLEANSING BATH:

The basic building blocks of any spiritual bath are water and salt. For the Catholics out there, think of Holy Water. Water alone contains the vital flow of life which has the ability to cleanse away spiritual obstacles. In ancient Babylonia, two types of water were known of as EA and AE. These two types of water were fresh water and sea water, or salt water. It has been said that these two waters have different qualities, spiritually speaking. Fresh water is used to sustain life, refresh us, and promote growth; while sea water or salt water was created to erase or dispel all evil and negative influences. Sea water or salt water has long been used since ancient times as the chief ingredient in most spiritual cleansing baths.

Also note that a spiritual cleansing bath is not the same as a physically cleansing bath, so I advise taking a bath or a shower for physical cleanliness first before doing the spiritual cleansing bath.

For creating an effective spiritual cleansing bath, add salt to your water. This can be sea salt, kosher salt, or table salt. Use one to three tablespoons. Hold the salt in your cupped hand and speak your prayer or intention into the salt, as if you were whispering a confidence into someone's ear, before pouring it into the water. In addition to the salt feel free to combine one or more of the common ingredients listed below which are reputed to carry the signature of spiritual cleansing. (Note if you use dried herbs, you may want to purchase reusable muslin bath tea bags, or a bath-sized, metal, mesh tea strainer to prevent the herbs from clogging the drain.) Also please make sure you are not allergic or sensitive to any of the items listed below before placing them into your bath!

½ cup Apple Cider Vinegar
1 TBS Baking Soda
Bay Leaf
Basil
1 handful of Epsom Salt
Eucalyptus
½ cup Florida Water
Hyssop
Lemon Grass
Mint
Marjoram
Rosemary

Angelica Root and Rue are also used by some but they can cause problems for those with sensitive skin. Rue is well known as a protective and cleansing herb but it is also known to cause severe phytophotodermatitis, so I would not recommend using it in any type of personal cleansing bath.

How to take a Spiritual Cleansing Bath:

The two simplest ways to take a spiritual cleansing bath is to choose your ingredients, charge them with universal energy and either add them to your bath water, or steep them separately in a pan of hot water.

Version One:

After you have added the chosen ingredients to your warm bath water, allow them to steep for five minutes before you get into the tub.

Get into the tub.

Hold your intention within your mind's eye, for instance you might visualize yourself with a bright and shiny aura.

Then submerge yourself for a moment (at least up to your shoulders.)

Optionally recite any intentions, prayers, incantations, psalms, affirmation, or statement to spirit related to the cleansing you are performing. Know that the words aren't as important as the meaning that they have to you. In the same way that different symbols can have different meanings to separate people, so do words have different meanings. Use words that are meaningful to you as these are the ones that will carry a higher vibration. (As you get to know your spirit guides, they are also getting to know you, and also getting to know the meaning of your words.)

Pour the bath water over yourself while you speak your words or silently visualize yourself being cleansed. As the water runs down your body, visualize all negative energy, thoughtforms, or attachments being washed downward and away.

Step out of the tub and open the drain. Visualize all negativity being carried away and exiting down the drain with the used bathwater.

Another option is to save a little of the used bath water (place a little in a cup), which now contains your essence, and then dispose of it in a ritual way which is sometimes called "sealing the work." The most common way to do this is by taking the cup of water to a crossroad and tossing it out toward the west while visualizing all negativity going away with the setting sun.

Version Two:

This can be done in the shower or in a bath tub.

Steep your chosen ingredients in a pan of warm water for five to ten minutes.

Allow the water to cool down to a comfortable temperature.

As in version one, optionally recite any intentions, prayers, incantations, psalms, affirmation, or statement to spirit related to the cleansing you are performing. Know that the words aren't as important as the meaning that they have to you. In the same way that different symbols can have different meanings to separate people, so do words have different meanings. Use words that are meaningful to you as these are the ones that will carry a higher vibration. (As you get to know your spirit guides, they are also getting to know you, and also getting to know the meaning of your words.)

Standing in the tub or shower, pour the prepared bath water from the pan over yourself while you speak your words or silently visualize yourself being cleansed. As the water runs down your body, visualize all negative energy, thoughtforms, or attachments being washed downward and away.

Step out of the tub and open the drain. Visualize all negativity being carried away and exiting down the drain with the used bathwater.

If you want to seal your cleansing work by taking a bit of the used water to a crossroad, close the drain to keep the water from escaping right away. Save a little of the used bath water which has come into contact with your body (place a little in a cup), to dispose of it in a ritual way which is sometimes called "sealing the work." The most common way to do this is by taking the cup of water to a crossroad and tossing it out toward the west while visualizing all negativity going away with the setting sun.

Some spirit workers recommend not toweling off by allowing yourself to air dry after getting out of the tub or shower. The purpose of this is to retain the essence of the cleansing bath on your skin as a way to get the maximum benefit. In my experience, I believe you will have created a wonderful spiritual cleansing for yourself whether you towel off or not.

CLEARING PSYCHIC DEBRIS FROM AN AREA OR SPACE

Any room or space where you routinely perform energy work, spell casting, energy raising, psychic readings, or spirit work will require routine spiritual cleansing in order to clear away the psychic debris resulting from these actions. Even if you don't engage in any of this type of work, chances are you will still need to occasionally cleanse space as psychic debris has a tendency to accumulate as a result of many common, day to day experiences, such as an area where a heated argument occurred, any place where emotional extremes were experienced, any place with a high-traffic area, and any time a person with negative intentions has entered the space.

Cleansing or clearing can range in their level of intensity from a light clearing by doing a simple smudging with a Sage stick to remove negative vibrations, to a powerful, full-on, old time cleansing to blast out a malevolent infestation of a home. More vigorous clearings are covered in Book Three. For now, we will just cover a basic spiritual cleansing of space for the more common forms of psychic debris and removal of lower vibration entities (sometimes referred to as astral nasties, or astral parasites.)

BASIC CLEANSING/ CLEARING VIA FUMIGATION

Certain botanicals carry powerful magical signatures for spiritual cleansing and protection and their natural strengths can be released in a number of ways. One way, using the elements of fire and air, is by burning and the use of fumigation. Burning certain botanicals releases their power into the air, and because the smoke permeates the air, it potentially reaches every facet of a room or a house. Cleansing by fumigation is still considered one of the most potent ways of clearing psychic and/ or spiritual debris.

To truly get an effective cleanse, the smoke should come into contact with all of the area you have targeted for clearing. So smoke it up and make sure that you direct the smoke into the area which is in most need of cleansing. I've listed some common botanicals used for cleansing via fumigation. I have listed them according to strength based on my experience and the experience of other spirit workers as recounted to me over the years. The list begins with lower strength and ends with the more powerful botanicals for cleansing space. (Of course this is my opinion based on my experiences- you're mileage may vary.)

Sweet grass
Cedar
Benzoin
Rosemary
Copal
Sage
Sandalwood
Palo Santo
Lemongrass
Hyssop
Eucalyptus
Dragon's Blood

Basil
Frankincense
Camphor

Purchase or create either a smudge stick, or self-lighting incense. Another method would be to burn the dried botanicals directly on smoldering incense charcoal. Always practice fire safety and burn charcoals or incense in a censer or other heatproof container.

Make sure that you use dried herbs and always charge your materials first.

Smudge sticks can be easily made by hanging your chosen herb to dry and then tying your bundle together with a natural string such as hemp to form your smudge stick.

You can create your own Cleanse & Clear Incense by combining one or more of the botanicals listed above, (or any other of your preferred herbs) with the self-lighting incense base listed below. (This incense base is also seen in Dream Work Chapter.)

Self Lighting Incense Base
1 part very fine, untreated (no chemicals!) sawdust. (I prefer Maple or Pine)
1/3 part Yellow Sandalwood Powder

1 to 2 tsp of Salt Peter (Per cup of Self-Lighting Incense Base- adjust proportion as needed.)
Blend well

Then Add:

2/3 part of your chosen finely ground and powdered herbs and or resins
Blend well.

Then Add:

1 dropper (per cup) of either a correlated single essential oil, or a correlated combination of essential oils and blend well once more

Note: I like to make my incense blends powdery but with a slightly moist texture. This makes it easy to simply grab a pinch of it with my fingers and place a cone-shaped deposit of incense onto my censer, ready to light.

Caution: Always be careful with Salt Peter as it is combustible around open flame.

To cleanse away any psychic or spiritual debris in a room, place your fire/ heat safe brazier in the center of the room. I like to use a small bucket of sand for this. Recite any intention or prayer, affirmation, or invitation to helpful spirits as you light the incense or smudge stick. Then address the four quarters of the room by systematically beginning in one section and then moving in a deosil or clock-wise direction, making sure you direct the smoke into the corners as you go around. You might want to use a feather or your hand to direct the smoke and make three passes as you go around.

Often an immediate effect will be noticed when you are done. The vibration will feel lighter and free of any tension or constraint.

Fumigation can also be done to cleanse an individual. This can be done by placing the fire and heat safe brazier on the floor and having the individual stand next to it while the smoke is wafted up and over the individual. If a smudge stick is used, simply walk around the person and direct the smoke to flow over them as you move around them.

A good basic cleansing can also be achieved by asperging or sprinkling charged water, such as consecrated salt and water, camphor and water, or Florida Water are some traditionally used substances. Used in a way similar to fumigation when clearing a room, charge your materials and start by reciting any intention or prayer, affirmation, or invitation to helpful spirits as you begin. Then address the four quarters of the room by systematically beginning in one section and then moving in a deosil or clock-wise direction, making sure you sprinkle into the corners as you go around.

A good way to seal the cleansed room is by embing protective symbols or sigils into the corners of the room and the doorway. This can be done by "drawing" your chosen symbol in the air with your finger in front of you and then using strong intention, pushing it with your hand into the space before you. Symbols used might be runes, Bindrunes, Icelandic runes, religious symbols, Reiki Symbols, Wiccan Symbols, or other magical or spiritual images depending on your beliefs and what you are warding from.

CHAPTER SIX
PSYCHIC CORDS

Psychic Cords are energetic attachments that are connected between two individuals' corresponding Chakras. Psychic cords are sometimes referred to as energetic binding or energy bonds and are created by the continuous discharge of intense emotional and/ or mental energy taking its course in one or more of the energetic layers of reality, such as the astral, etheric, spiritual, mental, or emotional planes. Psychic cords are formed from the energetic charge created when there is a time of increased mental and emotional energy focused on another person. These cords form a powerful connection transcending time and space, and will often remain even after death.

Like Indra's net, threads of psychic energy can be found running between ourselves and all of the people who have touched our lives. Many types of energetic connections, bonds, or cords exist. These cords can be positive or negative and brief or long-term. Psychic Cords can reach between the living and the dead, and can also remain intact through any spans of time, space, or planes of existence.

These cords cannot be seen by most people (but are quite often felt) and may be formed intentionally or unintentionally by *both* individuals. Most psychic cords start out positive and usually remain that way. Occasionally a psychic cord will start out negative and will usually remain negative. Sometimes cords change over time. A cord that started out positive can later turn negative and (although unlikely) a cord that started out negative could later turn positive! Just know that all cords are only able to manifest when both individuals agree on either a conscious or subconscious level. Some cords may last your entire life and possibly beyond, but many are more short term and will naturally dissolve or go dormant when they no longer serve the people connected.

Examples of Positive Cords

Examples of positive psychic cords are; cords between young children and parents which are vital to their survival- this type of cording may run between at least one, and possibly all seven major Chakras and allows the parents to be tuned into their infant or young child's needs. In love relationships between lovers, spouses, family, and close friends, positive Heart Chakra cords will be found. In loving and sexually intimate relationships you will find positive Heart Chakra cords and also positive Sacral Chakra cords.

Another type of positive cord is connected to the Solar Plexus Chakra between the physical body and the astral body and allows for safe astral travel to occur without injurious effects to the physical body. Positive cords are healthy and balanced and may appear anytime that two people choose, either consciously or subconsciously, to connect with each other for energetic and emotional support. Positive psychic cords will always be found between us and the people who matter most to us in our lives such as family, friends, lovers, and coworkers.

Examples of Negative Psychic Cords

Examples of negative psychic cords that have probably been intentionally or unintentionally negative since their beginning are any type of abusive or manipulative relationships, whether it is between two adults- such as an abusive husband or wife, or an abusive parent and child, or even an abusive work situation between a boss and employee. Along with poor personal boundaries, these negative energetic bonds are one of the most common ways we end up with other peoples' unwanted issues and energies invading our energetic (and sometimes physical) field and consequently draining our energy. Alcoholism, drug addiction, low self-esteem, codependency, and internalized shame can create an environment ripe for the birthing of negative psychic cords.

An important factor to remember is that on either a conscious or subconscious level, both individuals have to agree for this negative cord to manifest. The contributing reasons for this to occur are wide and varied but factors such as low self esteem, guilt, a need to be needed, a need to control, or a more malignant driving force could be the need for one of the individuals to feel powerful.

Sadly, the underlying drive or root cause behind intentional negative cords are often an attempt to control or manipulate another person's thoughts, feelings, or behaviors. Sometimes if the intentional corder does not want to be found out they may attach negative cords to the back (back chakra) of another person's body. This type of cording signals danger and warns of a corder with a deceptive nature and treacherous intent.

Examples of Positive Cords that Stagnate or turn Negative

Usually when a cord is no longer desired, or needed by the two people involved, it will naturally go dormant or disconnect itself. Sometimes problems arise when a positive psychic cord has concluded its natural course and remains attached either intentionally or unintentionally due to one of the individuals' resisting the disconnection. This unbalanced situation sets up an unhealthy situation for the individual that is wishing to disconnect.

A prime example of psychic cords which were initially positive but later turned negative are at the end of any love relationship that is breaking apart, and one of the individuals does not want this to happen and refuses to let go.

Another example occurs in parent and adult child relationship where the parent retains an unhealthy desire for control, or an adult child is overly dependent and resists taking on adult responsibilities. Often a negative or distorted Solar Plexus Chakra cords will be found.

A cord which was initially positive and later turned negative might also be seen in some types of personal or business relationships which started out positive but later ends and one of the individuals is unwilling to move on. I had this happen some years ago with a coworker that I befriended and trusted, who later, unbeknownst to me began a series of hurtful, underhanded behaviors directed at me in the work place. I knew something was wrong but she would always deny any problems when asked. During this stretch of time I experienced a steadily deteriorating immune system. I was getting sick all the time and my energy always seemed drained. Although I suspected, I did not want to believe that this person had negative intentions toward me. I was somewhat naïve and did not realize the extent of her hate until a number of other coworkers came forward to tell me what she was doing. Not long afterwards, while performing an energy scan on myself, I was able to sense very clearly a large, negative cord attached to one of my back chakras. I was able to dissolve this cord and surround myself with protection after this. This was my only time experiencing a negative back corder who did not want to be found out. I also moved to another shift afterwards to distance myself from the toxic behavior.

Other examples of Psychic Cords

Psychic cords of brief duration may form temporarily numerous times over the course of our lives. One example of a short term psychic cord is one that is formed during a working relationship on a time-limited project. Most long lasting psychic cords occur between family, friends, and other significant persons in our life.

Sometimes a psychic cord will outlast our lifetime, transcending time and space. A cord of connection often runs through our ancestral line. Also in past lives we may have established powerful bonds which still exist in our current lifetime. This type of psychic cord may have no untoward effect, or it may cause what some call a "Past Life Intrusion." A Past Life Intrusion is when the effect of a traumatic event or a psychic cord/ bond from a past life spills over into the present day life.

One example of a past life intrusion happened with a client's daughter who was engaged to be married when she began experiencing intense dreams of another man. The recurring dreams started out somewhat sweet and benign but somewhere along the line these dreams took a negative turn. The source of these dreams which later turned nightmarish turned out to be a man that she had been engaged to from a past life. In this case, dissolving the psychic cord which connected them helped but it was only after doing a past life healing session that enabled complete closure to happen. (More on past life healing in Chapter Ten.)

It's interesting to note that intrusions from past life cords are usually triggered when the individual becomes the same age that the past event occurred or have present day circumstances currently manifesting which mirror the past life event.

HOW TO DETECT PSYCHIC CORDS

Psychic cords can be found a few different ways. If you are good at visualization, you may be able to sense them this way. Some folks who are better at kinesthetically sensing energy may run their hands close to the body and sense a change in energy which is felt through their hands. Some of you may get your best information by using a pendulum to dowse. Others may be able to systematically run focus through the body and sense any blocks, or anywhere a sense of pulling or tension is detected. Call upon your spirit guides to aid your clarity, provide extra insight or information, or to help you through the process of detecting and dissolving negative psychic cords.

Psychic cords are frequently described as cables, roots, or as resembling umbilical cords and may be anchored with hooks or roots. Healthy positive cords are usually sensed to be robust, thick, and vibrant with energy that most often flows both ways. It is always important to sense which direction the energy is flowing. Positive psychic cords are usually pink, tan, gold, or white. If the psychic cord is thin, dark, and contains no energy it is probably an old cord that is no longer active.

Negative cords can also be just as robust as positive ones but the color and energy flow differ. Negative psychic cords may be gray, black, or occasionally an angry red. The energy may only run one way or in a very unbalanced way. Negative cords will likely reconnect after being disconnected unless you take steps to protect your Chakras.

It's possible to have a positive and a negative cord with the same person. If you find this happening, you will probably only want to disconnect the negative cord.

DETECTING A NEGATIVE CORD:

The hallmark sign of having a negative cord attachment is feeling physically and emotionally drained by another person. Other symptoms that may be experienced are a tense or pulling sensation at the connection point; feeling ungrounded; feeling unbalanced; problems with sleep, meditation, or clear thinking. Over time a negative cord attachment can compromise your physical health and immune system due to emotional and energetic draining. Upon reflection, most of us who have a negative cord attachment will usually sense or "know" on some level that it is there.

Block out some time where you will be undisturbed and get into a quiet space. (Thirty minutes is usually an adequate amount of time.) To determine if you have a negative cord attachment, get yourself into a relaxed state. Set your intention to "see" or sense all psychic cords or connections to your major chakras. Ground and center yourself. Ask the Universal Energy to flow through you.

You may want to ask your healing guides or allies to assist you. Scan your energy body, or if you are guiding someone else direct them to do so at this time. There is more than one way to access the information. If you are not getting the information at this point you might find it helpful to step into the Void and ask your guide to directly show you what you need to see or you may want to employ the aid of psychic tools as outlined below. Experiment a little and see what works best for you.

As you receive the information, observe how the cord looks or feels and discern if it is a negative or positive cord. (Remember it is possible to have both types of cords with one person.) If it is a positive cord, it will look bright, may often show up it pink, tan, white or gold colors and have a healthy "feel" to it. If it is a negative cord, it will have an unhealthy feel to it and is often a discolored or putrid green, dusky gray, black, or sometimes an angry red in color.

Next visualize the person you suspect of having a negative cord attachment with you. If you don't know who it is, before becoming entirely relaxed, set your intention that you be shown who the person is.

If you have had interactions with this person, bring to mind the last time you were in contact with this person and carefully note the way you feel. Did you experience an energy drain, any stress, or any negative or distressing emotions? If this is an unfamiliar person that you are being shown, how did you feel when you sensed that person? Did you feel a positive, neutral, or negative reaction? If you had any sense of energy draining, stressful or distressing emotions, or any other negative reactions to the known or unknown person continue to the next step.

Ask yourself to sense or remember how long have these reactions or feelings been with you? If you find that it has been over a long period of time, then it is very likely that you have a negative psychic cord attachment. The reason to determine how long this has been going on is that there is often the possibility due to day to day stressors, for temporary negative cords of brief duration to form and dissolve all on their own. These types of cords can arise from conflict with others, or other stressful conditions and are always temporary and can even sometimes be a factor in contributing to our own growth and development.

USE OF PSYCHIC TOOLS TO DETECT CORDS:

The use of psychic tools can be helpful if for some reason you are unable to determine if a negative psychic cord exists, or tools can be used as a way of confirming the impressions received while going through the process of sensing and detecting a negative cord.

Pendulum: A pendulum can be used to detect or confirm the presence of a negative psychic cord. First, make sure your pendulum is cleansed of any previous influence. This can be accomplished by either submersion into salt or salt water (make sure it will not damage the pendulum) or by permeating it with the smoke of a cleansing botanical, such as Frankincense, Sage, or Basil. If you use salt water, leave it submerged for a minute or two, rinse it off under running water, and then wipe dry with a paper towel or clean cloth.

Program the pendulum to establish a simple means of communication. Do this by holding the pendulum between both of your hands and charging it with your energy. Then before you begin hold a clear picture in your mind of what motion means "yes" and what motion means "no." Some people consider it a yes for vertical movement and a no for horizontal movement. I do it this way because that is the way my head moves with a nod for yes, and a side to side movement for no. Other folks use clockwise movement verses counter-clockwise movement for either yes/ no answers or to gage the energy flow of chakras. Use whatever feels right to you, but have it set in your mind ahead of time.

To begin, relax your mind. Focus on one major chakra at a time and ask your question. You might focus on the Root Chakra and ask: are any negative cords present? And then proceed to the next chakra with your focus and intention while asking the question again. Continue in this way until you have screened each major chakra.

Tarot: Using the **Seven Chakra Spread** below can be useful in detecting an interruption in the flow of energy. This interruption could be due to the presence of a negative psychic cord or the cards may reveal other influences affecting your energy. Lay the cards out as shown below, with each card representing the associated chakra. So card number one represents the Root Chakra, card two represents the Sacral Chakra, card three represents the Solar Plexus Chakra, card four represents the Heart Chakra, card five represents the Throat Chakra, card six represents the Third Eye Chakra, and card seven represents the Crown Chakra.

7
6
5
4
3
2
1

Some of you may even find it beneficial to use both tools. One way of doing this might be to use your tarot cards for a Seven Chakra Spread and then position the pendulum over any questionable cards to further clarify the information.

PSYCHIC SURGERY

Psychic Surgery is the action of sensing, removing and clearing psychic debris from an individual. This is not physical surgery. Psychic Surgery, as it is described in this book, is something that you could do alone or in conjunction with another person as a way to dissolve negative cords and can also be used to remove spirit attachments (more on spirit attachments in Book Three.) The act of dissolving a negative cord will often also serve to release old resentments, old family issues, old pain related to past issues trauma and abuse, and old hurts or anger which provided fuel for the cord to manifest and remain in place. There are many forms of Psychic Surgery, but one form of Psychic Surgery that we will discuss here is the dissolution of *negative energy cords*.

If you have detected a negative psychic cord by one of the methods listed above, then proceed to the next phase by holding a session to dissolve the negative psychic cord. The session outlined below can be used on yourself or to guide another person in dissolving a negative cord. If you have negative psychic cords connecting you to more than one person, it is recommended that you hold a separate session for each person. Knowing what caused the negative cord to form is helpful in the healing process but it isn't necessary to dissolve or sever a negative cord. Sometimes we will receive insight as to why the cord formed, and sometimes we won't. Sometimes we only receive insight into how it formed after the cord has been dissolved. In any case this is okay. Don't allow yourself to become stuck in the trap of wanting to understand the "why" if the insight isn't readily apparent. Sometimes the presence of a negative psychic cord can "fog up the glass" so much that we may not be able to see clearly. In other words, don't delay the elimination of a negative cord just because you don't understand it. Just know that a negative psychic cord will always be detrimental to you the longer it remains.

DISSOLVING NEGATIVE PSYCHIC CORD SESSION:

Perform this session after the detection of a negative psychic cord.

Optional, but I recommend taking a cleansing bath or shower using sea salt prior to beginning. Block out some undisturbed time in your meditation area to complete this process.

Hang up the Do Not Disturb Sign and get into a quiet space. (Thirty minutes is usually an adequate amount of time.)

Focus on your breathing, take some deep cleansing breaths, and get yourself into a relaxed state.

Set your intention to "see" or sense all psychic cords or connections to your major chakras. Ground and center yourself. Ask the Universal Energy to flow through you. Surround yourself with a sphere of protective light.

Ask the Highest Divine Power of your understanding to allow healing energy to flow through you, and to guide and protect you during this session.

If you are working with any other helpful, allied spirits such as your Spirit Guide, Healing Guide, Ancestral Guide, Guardian Angel, or other Spirit Allies you may want to call upon them also to add clarity, insight, or extra information regarding the Negative Psychic Cord during this session.

Take a deep slow cleansing breath and close your eyes if you have not already done so. Proceed onward when you feel ready.

Allow yourself to see, feel, or sense the negative cord attached to you. Follow the cord to see where it leads. Can you sense the other person? Does this negative cord connect to one of their chakras? (This will usually be the other person's corresponding chakra.)

See if there is a cord extending from a Chakra of this person connecting to one of your corresponding chakras. Take note of its appearance and/ or how it feels. (At this stage, if a negative cord is not detected, or if you find a positive cord, then take a couple cleansing breaths and end the process. Otherwise continue onward.)

Ask questions to figure out what you are dealing with.
What does the cord look like?
What color is it?
Is it thick or thin? (Usually the longer it has been there, the thicker it is.)
Is it filled with energy?
Which way is the energy flowing?
Does the energy flow to you or away from you?
Who is the person is at the other end?
What is going on with the other person?
If you are able to, try to look past the other person's layers and into their core. Negative cords are frequently formed from a base of fear or pain and covered by anger or an unhealthy need to control the other person.
Continue onward if you detect a negative cord.

Surround the other person in a sphere of protective light to contain their energy. Sense their reaction, if any, and let them know that they will not be harmed during this process.

Ask that any information that you need to know about the other person and the manifestation of this cord come to you at this time.

Silently or out loud communicate your intention to dissolve this negative cord running between you and the other person. You might want to take the time to say any words about this negative connection that you may not have been able to say in the past. If you are able to end with forgiveness know that it can be very healing. (Forgiveness is a tool for healing and is never interpreted as saying what the other person may have done is "okay" in any way, just that it no longer holds power over you.) If you are unable to forgive, that is alright, keep going!

Examine your conscious, if you have any resentment or if you are holding on to any old pains, hurts, anger, or fear towards this person, now is the time to release them.

Ask your spirit guide/s to take any old hurts, pains, or fears to take these from you and the other person as the cord is dissolved. You can make a statement regarding this or just set the intention.

As you begin to dissolve this negative cord sense the Universal Energy flowing through you, and power up the focus on your intention of dissolving or severing the cord. See your intention form into laser-like beam of golden light. In your mind's eye see or sense the laser breaking the cord apart as it dissolves and falls away from both you and the other person's chakras. At the same time you see any or all emotional and mental baggage related to the formation of this cord (fear, anger, stress, guilt, regret, hurt, battered self-esteem) fall away.

The area where the cord was connected to your chakra is now empty. Nature abhors a vacuum and will attempt to fill it up. Do not leave this space empty! It could fill up with unwanted energy, another cord, or an entity. Holding your hands over the space, visualize the Universal Energy flowing through you, cleansing, protecting, and then filling the empty space with golden white light. Emb it, or seal the energy in with your intention for the highest good and for the healing of yourself and the other person.

You now need to do the same thing for the other person. Take the same steps, in the same order; if any cord remains on their end, dissolve it with the same focused intent. Then hold your hands over their space, visualize the universal healing energy flowing through you, cleansing, protecting, and then filling their empty space with golden white light. Observe any reaction or response from this other person. To separate your two energies, visualize the other person who is still within the protective sphere being moving further and further away, until you can no longer see them.

You are now free of the negative cord attachment. When you feel ready, take a deep breath and open your eyes. The session is complete.

PROTECTION AGAINST RE-CORDING

Be sure to take precautions against re-cording. Often times after dissolving a negative psychic cord the other person may sense what has happened on an energetic or subconscious level and, in desperation may attempt to reconnect the cord. At the very least, this person will sense a change in you and they will most likely feel very uncomfortable around you. It is not uncommon to find that they may call or try to visit you in the hours or days following the cord disconnection. Some psychologists term this as "change back" behaviors. The simplest plan would be to discontinue all contact with them. Many times this might not be possible; especially if the other person is someone you are required to deal with in your day to day life following the negative cord disconnection, such as a close family member, or someone that you work with. If this is the case, take it as a personal challenge to yourself as part of your own spiritual growth process.

The best way to prevent negative cord reconnection is to try to live each day to your ideal best, while knowing that you will never be perfect, always striving to do the "next right thing." Listen to your inner voice. If you have trusted guides, you may allow yourself to be "spirit led" when unsure about how to proceed with someone. The best precautions to have in place beyond this is to routinely practice clearing your energy field by clearing, strengthening, and balancing your chakras, and also surrounding yourself with protection. This is particularly true prior to anytime you may come into contact with person that you had been connected to with a negative cord.

Clearing, Strengthening, & Balancing Your Chakras:

Get into a comfortable position by sitting or lying down. With your inner vision, starting with the Root Chakra and moving upward through the Major Chakras, see or sense each chakra and their colors; Root Chakra/ red, Sacral Chakra/ orange, Solar Plexus Chakra/ yellow, Heart Chakra/ green, Throat Chakra/ blue, Third Eye Chakra/ Indigo, and Crown Chakra/ lavender to white; see or sense each chakra.

Pause at each chakra to determine; are there any darkened areas, or murky energy?
As your inner vision travels through each chakra, see or sense the energy center becoming more clear and vibrant. When they are all clear, see or sense each chakra filling with energy and spinning clockwise at peak effectiveness, at an effortless pace.
Before you end, see or sense all of your chakras spinning at the same speed and in sync with each other.

Energy Field/ Chakra Protection:

The simplest way, and the way to protect all your major chakras, and your entire energy field is to visualize, see or sense your entire being surrounded in a sphere of protective golden-white light. You can make this as layered or as elaborate as you like. You may emb protective symbols into it, you may form it in the sense of a shield or a grid system, or anything else you sense powers up your protective field. The important thing is to do it. The more often you build this energetic field, the stronger and more effective it will be. Doing it daily is a great habit to get into. It is especially vital, not only after the disconnection of negative psychic cords, but also prior to doing any spirit work.

Other aspects to consider adding to you protective energy field may include placing extra protective elements over the chakra areas that previously had negative cord attachments. This could be visualizing protective mirrors covering and reflecting outward from the chakra. Some folks may visualize or use crystals (More on this in the upcoming Spirit Worker's Book on Stones & Crystals) over specific chakras to protect, cleanse, or to keep them balanced. There are many ways to protect and strengthen vulnerable areas within the energy field. It's best to try a few different ways and see what works best for you.

SHADOW

My shadow tells a story
Of survival through dark nights
As the lost pieces come together
I journey into light

My shadow tells a story
Of old outrage filled with pain
I gaze into my shadow's eyes
Where secrets still remain

My shadow tells a story
No longer filled with fear
I reach out to take her hand
Together we are here

My shadow tells a story
As we dance beneath the moon
Our magical transformation
Rising from primal ruins

My shadow tells a story
Of survival through the night
Our journey takes us through the stars
Unified in flight

DV

CHAPTER SEVEN
SHADOW WORK

WHAT IS A SHADOW?

The most common definition of a human "shadow" is that the shadow is made up of the parts of yourself which you try to deny, hide, control, or suppress because these qualities are unacceptable to you. But that's not the whole story, your shadow is made up of much more than these perceived negative attributes.

In shamanic witchcraft and other shamanic spirit work, facing your shadow is necessary and usually one of our greatest challenges.

You will never totally get rid of your shadow, and you don't need to. Shadow work is not about getting rid of the shadow, it's about making it healthy and balanced. A heavy shadow is often what holds us back in life, no matter its origins! Yes, our shadow is made up of some of the "negative" aspects of self, but it also contains the positive aspects which have to do with your intuition and inner knowing. The benefit of doing shadow work is that the more you clear away or transform the negative or dysfunctional aspects, the more in touch you will become with your deep, inner well of knowledge which is also your shadow. Shadow work ultimately brings you into balance with what your shadow was meant to be.

You may be consciously or subconsciously suppressing shadow aspects and the perception of these qualities may be "good" or "bad." Negative shadow aspects are usually born out of a traumatic experience, and are created by you as a way to adapt or cope. Sometimes these troublesome shadow aspects may have been brought about by the conditioning influence of those around you when you were a young child. In any case, continuing on the path of victim is never a healthy choice. It is up to you to heal or deal with your own shadow. We can't change the past. We can't even change what happened five minutes ago, but we can change what we are doing from this moment forward. The choice is ours and that choice is the root of your power.

In the chapters regarding shadow work, I focus on the healing of negative aspects of shadow self because this is the thing that most often hampers spirit work. The positive aspects of shadow aren't going to give you any problems!

Everyone has shadow aspects. The important thing to know about heavy or negative shadow aspects is that they can rob you of your personal power. But another important thing to know is that you can take that power back at any time. Also, I recommend not delving deeper into any type of spirit work where you may encounter malevolent beings unless you have done the footwork of keeping yourself in reasonably good spiritual condition.

There is something of a debate among the community of self-help types of folks around the issue of what exactly is the best thing to do with your shadow aspects. Some would argue that positive affirmations work best. Others may say that going to the root cause is the only way to become spiritually "woke." Others may say the only way to heal or integrate shadow aspects is by taking the blue pill instead of the red. My belief is that all of the different techniques to "wellness" have merit and the best way to go about Shadow Work is to use what works best for you. Shadow work is part of the process of getting to know you, the "good" and the "bad."

What you will find in this book are suggestions. It will be up to you to "try them on" and decide what works for you.

Real personal power builds within you when you are not giving away your power. One of the major red flags of a shadow aspect rearing its ugly little head is when we react to something or someone with highly charged negative emotional energy. If you find that you have a strong negative reaction to another person, it is usually because this person is reflecting your own shadow aspect back to you. You are seeing in this person the very thing which you do not want to acknowledge in yourself.

As you begin this journey of self-discovery, I hope you realize that you are your own personal mystery school. This journey of personal gnosis begins with coming to understand your shadow. Shadow work is not done for the purpose of picking apart all of the horrible little things about you, but it is about being honest with yourself. It is not done to self-help yourself to death, or to "perfect" your personality. Shadow work is really about integrating or coming to terms with, and hopefully coming to love (or at least accept), the parts of yourself that you could not accept before. To do that you first need to be honest with exactly what your shadow is.

HOW TO IDENTIFY YOUR SHADOW ASPECT

The easiest way to identify your shadow aspects is to make a simple list. What trips your trigger on a routine basis? Identify shadow by making a simple list of the things we find undesirable in ourselves. This list should be kept ultra simple. You don't want to go into this process with the intention of psychoanalyzing yourself to death because that is a trap. I'm not saying you should ignore the past, but you don't want to dwell in the past either. Reliving old traumas, hurts or shame more than once creates a trail or spiral of pain that grows deeper and wider each time you re-experience it. Don't allow yourself to feed the beast by getting stuck on the "why." In other words, accept the fact that you might never understand why your mom set you on the potty sideways and move on. So keep the list simple.

A shadow aspect develops in response to a threat to either one of our expectations, or to one of the basic instincts of life. Our basic instincts of life usually fall into one of two very broad categories: security instincts or our social instincts. The social instinct is usually related to issues of self-esteem or personal relationships. The security instinct is usually related to material, physical, and emotional well-being, and ambitions.

Sometimes we may need to do more than just identify our shadow parts; sometimes we may need to do a little footwork. For instance, we might identify an aspect of false pride and then do the footwork to make a decision to act/ re-act the opposite way- which might be – being humble, being able to ask for help, or admitting that we are not always right. If the problem was fear, we might want to choose to act "as if" we had courage instead. If the problem is with anger- know that anger always comes from a perceived threat to one of your basic instincts of life. Also know that just about every negative emotional issue can be linked to the problem of misdirected instinct. As human beings our instincts are a vital and important part of our make-up. We all have desires for love, sex, companionship, and emotional and material security. It is when we warp these desires that we develop the Shadow aspects of self.

Shadow work is never about beating yourself up. One of the highest forms of self-love might be to just take a look within and do what we can to either live with or transform the shadow parts of self. Will we ever be perfect? I'm sure you know the answer is no. But that shouldn't deter us from doing the internal work. It is the process of doing the work, not so much the outcome which can propel us to awakening in spirit.

All of us have issues which we would rather not think about, such as low self esteem, feelings of inadequacy, fears of not getting what we want, or fears of losing what we've got, jealousy, selfishness, and on and on. So what! Clear out the cobwebs and take a look at what goes on inside of you. Starting to do this will automatically decrease the power any shadow aspect has over you.

Possible Indicators of Shadow
(Remember that these are just possible indicators of shadow aspects. Most often you will feel fine and then suddenly find yourself "triggered" into a negative space within you.)

Issues with self-esteem

Feeling that you are not good enough
Chronic issues with personal relationships
Holding onto or re-experiencing old trauma, hurt, or fear
Over-reacting
Experiencing extreme negative emotions in response to a non-extreme person or circumstance
Judging others
Chronic guilt
Unhealthy Shame
Being dishonest with others
Being dishonest with yourself
Being intolerant
Always comparing yourself to others
Hanging onto anger or resentments
Hate
Self-Pity
Chronic Self-Centered-ness (the world according to me! aka the *"Me First"* syndrome)
Extreme procrastination, feeling stuck, feeling unable to take action or move forward in life

I'm sure I could make an endless list, but you pretty much get the picture. We all experience these things on the list from time to time but if it is something that you trip over on a day to day or frequent basis, you probably need to take a closer look.

SAFETY PRECAUTIONS

There are shadows and then there are *Shadows*. Everybody is different and unique. What works for one individual may not help as much for another individual. Some of our shadow aspects may cast a small shadow, while others may truly cast a much larger shadow. That is why I don't necessarily buy into the concept of making "friends" with your shadow. Some of us may be able to "make friends" but for others a shadow unchecked has the power and the potential to actually kill us or bring true harm to those around us. We are each unique and different. Our shadows will never totally go away, but we can learn how to transform them or work with them. Self-accountability is key.

Those of us with smaller shadow aspects may feel more annoyed with ourselves when a shadow aspect makes itself known. Maybe even shrugging off its presence with saying, "you again?" Those of us with more powerful shadows can make the choice to practice shadow work. If you engage in shadow work, even if you have a strong shadow aspect, you will see results. Your shadow will be transformed or transmuted. I've seen it work for many people who probably had much bigger shadows than you.

The best spiritual defense you can ever hope to have is to be spiritually healthy and spiritually centered. If your spiritual house is in order, everything else in your life and in your work will fall into place.

White light visualizations and its many variations will not do much good if your own spiritual affairs are not in order. Take the time to assess your soul. If you are doing things that on some level you know are not good for you or the people around you, all the white light in the world is not going to protect you from psychic or spiritual attack. You have compromised yourself, and by compromising yourself you have cut off your spiritual connection to any higher power, making it easier for lower powers to enter.

Signs of a shadow might take the form of rehashing an event or a problem that you've had with another person over and over again in your head. When you do this, all of your energy is going into the re-thinking, re-feeling, or re-experiencing of this event and there is no room left inside of you for spirit to connect with you. Try to be aware of anything that is taking up space inside of you, anything that occupies a space in your mind or in your heart. If you are filled up with these types of thoughts and feelings it can cause an inability to connect with benevolent spirits. Not only will you experience difficulty in connecting to higher vibration spirits, but you may also have a difficult time connecting with your own spirit! You'll know. If you are having trouble connecting to spirit, or perhaps you are feeling disconnected, spiritually numb, and/ or cut off from your own spirit, then it is time to take stock. So be very careful. Take a look at what are the main things are that you think about or focus on in your day to day life?

The two main offenders that crop up are resentments over past hurts or harms and fear. Resentment has to do with focusing on past events and fear is usually heightened anxiety about the future. Neither of these negative emotional states serves us here in our spiritual lives or in our day to day physical lives. Remember, if you have one foot in yesterday and the other foot in tomorrow, you are pissing on today!

So some examples of shadow aspects might be having something that your parents did to you ten years ago is rehashed in your mind every other day and begins to drive your decision making process, or maybe something that your boyfriend or girlfriend did to you last week is starting to occupy and consume your thoughts during your quiet times. Whatever it is, find a way to let it go. That's toxic to the soul and the thing is the more space that is taken up inside of you rehashing old hurts and betrayals, the more cut off from spirit you become! The old traumas, hurts, and fears fill you up and you simply have no inner space left for spirit to connect with you.

I know, I know, you're probably saying, yeah but what about the situations where we were wronged! What about that? My hurt and anger is very justified! Yeah, maybe it is, but I know from experience that a justified shadow aspect can grow into an old and cold resentment and it will take up permanent residence within a person's soul, cutting them off from spirit just as much as an unjustified shadow aspect.

You've got to find a way to get rid of that stuff, or it will hold you in bondage for the rest of your life and you will have given away all of your power to it. Not only that, but you will have also given the people contributing to the development of your shadow, the power to kill you! No joke, filling you or only a part of yourself up with shadow aspects, wreaks havoc not only on your soul but also on your physical health! If you are carrying some of this old toxic stuff, ask spirit to take it from you. And know that the "best revenge" is to live a wonderful life. Do whatever you need to do to move beyond it.

In much of spirit work you will come across a wide variety of lesser malignant entities that are nowhere close to demonic in nature. Clearing parasites or low-lying entities is usually par for the course but when you come into dealing with intelligent, complex malevolent beings; you are operating on a whole different level. You cannot sage them away. The work is dangerous and not for the faint-hearted. Most spirit workers that have worked in the realm of spirit release and exorcism will recommend not doing this work if you have children at home or other vulnerable family members. There are matters to consider before you head down the path of this work. Broker no illusions around the practice of spirit work.

As a recovering alcoholic, who has worked a 12-Step program for many years, I see the 12 Steps as taking the most powerful practices of all the world's religions and spiritual practices, and breaking them down into baby-food so that somebody like me can understand the principles behind them. The whole process of Surrender – Taking Inventory - Clearing House - Getting Right with everyone around you - & Awakening to and Maintaining Conscious Contact with a Higher Power, is the only process I can think of that is anywhere close to the best practices recommended before doing the work of Spirit Release, Spirit Rescue, Exorcism, or similar related spirit work. If any of you are in recovery I'm sure you will see the parallels in what I am writing.

Once you have dealt with any residual spiritual matters within yourself, anything that you do for spiritual protection will work better because even if you don't realize it initially, you have opened yourself up enough to connect with higher powered spiritual allies. Spiritual white light and cleansing baths work much better, or begin to work when they haven't worked in the past.

So once your spiritual house is in order; have at it with a simple protective white light and/ or spiritual cleansings. No more lecturing!

KEY STEPS TO SHADOW WORK

Identify your shadow aspects (who or what triggers or upsets us?)

Indentify what is affected (who or what is perceived as a threat to a personal relationship, a threat to job or income, a threat to well-being, etc.)

Identify the nature of your shadow (Fear, anger, dishonesty, selfishness, being judgmental etc.)

Become willing to release or transform the Shadow Aspect

Ask (in whatever form you sense the highest energy of Divine spirit) **to take this Shadow Aspect and transform it into a higher, more useful energy**

Work with Spirit, but also *you* need to do the footwork to transform this shadow by doing the *opposite* of what the shadow energy is. (No spirit, the big S or the little s, will do for us what we can do for ourselves. This is a form of acting *"as if,"* So counter dishonesty by being honest/ selfishness by being unselfish / judging others by practicing being accepting or tolerant)

SURRENDERING THE INNER SHADOW

You will need to find a way of looking at the different aspects of you. Sometimes this can be as simple as making a list. Write down the positive and the negative traits within you.

You do not need to show this to anybody but often the act of just taking something out of yourself, out of your head, and writing it down on paper can make a big difference. Often we have blind spots and don't realize what those parts of ourselves are doing to us. Sometimes just being able to acknowledge what these hidden traits are can be enough to draw the more undesirable parts of ourselves out into the light where they either wither and die or transform.

Some folks may only need to go through this process once, coming out the other side of it truly changed. I suspect that for most of us there will be a few "go rounds" as we journey through life's many transitions, before arriving at a state of reconciliation within the self- if ever.

You may ask, why go through the process at all? What is the purpose of it? Some valuable reasons for undertaking a process of surrender and awakening in relationship to any sort of Spirit Work is that your body, mind, and soul will fare better and be more effective if you are not struggling with the Shadow aspects of self, which is something we all have.

Also know that if your work later leads to encounters with malevolent tricksters or any demonic beings, many of them have the extremely annoying ability to read your thoughts right down to the deepest, darkest corners of your psyche.

So it is highly recommended that if you have not previously done so, that you "clean house" *especially* before undertaking deeper aspects of spirit work such as spirit release, protection, or exorcism work (more on that in Book Three of the Spirit Work Series.) What follows in the next chapter are some simplistic ways of lightning up, transforming, or at least making friends with your shadow. One way to start the process of getting rid of any old baggage is to go into vision. Some of you may find it helpful to begin by making a list of any old hurts or fears that you would like to be free of as these are usually the ingredients of shadow making.

SHADOW WORK TAROT SPREAD

This spread is not so much diagnostic as it is to provide extra insight into your shadow and to help provide some direction in your shadow work. Remember the cards are only a tool capturing a snapshot in time. If you see something you don't like in the cards, use it as information on making a better choice. Nothing is set in stone! Your life is shaped by your choices.

HEART OF THE SHADOW SPREAD

Shuffle the cards while thinking about any issues surrounding your shadow work. Cut the deck once and lay the cards out in the order shown below. This spread reveals the heart of the matter, as well as the symptoms, actions to take, and most likely outcome.

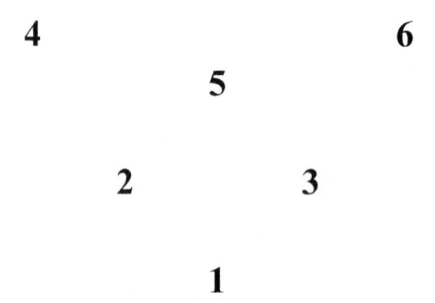

```
4                    6
         5

    2         3

         1
```

Card 1: Root- Reveals the heart of the issue

Card 2 & 3: Symptoms- indicates how this shadow aspect is currently manifesting in your life

Card 4: What's Needed- What you need at this time to aid the healing of your shadow

Card 5: Action- What action will help best in your shadow work

Card 6: Outcome- Shadow work requires growth and change. This card indicates how you will be different after healing and or transformational work.

CHAPTER EIGHT
INTO THE SHADOW

In this chapter are listed a few simple methods for examining, transforming, and/ or accepting the shadow aspects of self. The nuts and bolts of shadow work will usually begin as an inside job. Later on you may find that some external work might be necessary. Each of us is unique, carrying different experiences with us that have culminated into the person we are today. There are no musts! The different aspects of Shadow Work listed here are suggestions to help you find what works best for you. You might try all of them or you may want to just work with one or two of the suggested exercises.

One very simple way to get in touch with your shadow aspects is to grab paper and pen and make a list or start journaling. What you write is private and nobody else needs to see it. You might want to start with the simple Inventory Vision listed below.

BASIC INVENTORY VISION

Get into a relaxed state by taking a few deep, cleansing breaths. Close your eyes and quiet your mind. Use your imagination and see the inside of yourself as a store. It can be any kind of store. You might want a fancy one that sells fashionable handbags and shoes, or your store can be one of those little quick, convenience marts.

Allow yourself to look around your store to see what it is stocked up with. What is currently filling your shelves? Are there any out of date items or beliefs? Could there be some shelves that have spoiled goods stored on them? Are there some things just taking up shelf space so that you can't put anything new there?

Find any of the things in your "store" that you no longer want or need and start clearing off some of the shelves. Take any out-dated ways of thinking and toss them away. Clear out any attachments to anger, pain, fear, or bitterness. Allow yourself to remove anything negative inside of you. Know that any of these negative things that fill you up takes away from the valuable space available within you that could be filled instead with courage, hope, happiness, and a connection to Spirit. If you are filled up with too much of that stuff (unwanted thoughts and emotions), spirit is not able to get in there to connect with you because there is simply no room.

Take your time. You may want to go through this exercise a few times as we often have "blind spots." (I know I certainly do!) Write down your thoughts, feelings, and impressions.

Put it aside in a safe place where no one else will have access to your private journaling. Wait a day or two and then read through what you wrote, giving yourself time to reflect. Document any of your insights or new thoughts.

PERSONIFICATION OF SHADOW VISION

Another way to process some of your shadow self is to form a mental image of the shadow aspects of self. See these images swirling around until they finally come into a personified being that is similar to your whole self. This personified shape will no doubt look like you but with an amplification of the Shadow. An example might be, if shadow was filled with anger, you might see an image of self that has deep creases within their face; perhaps one that carries their body like a tightly coiled spring with flaming eyes that may have daggers shooting out of them. A shadow of false pride or an inflated sense of self may appear to be you with your nose in the air while walking around with a puffed out chest.

Many of these are negative remnants of survival which no longer serve you. Look into the ***eyes*** of this shadow and allow your-self to see the ***pain and fear*** underlying this shadow self. Let your shadow know that it's ok, that it's safe, and that they no longer need to be in this state. From here you may do whatever feels right- you may see yourself and the shadow breaking the chains that bind them, or you may want to give your shadow a hug and tell them that they will be alright. If there are any psychic cords attached to these images, see them dissolving or cut them away. Do whatever feels right to you at this time. When you feel ready, allow all aspects of yourself to be back within you.

Afterwards, take the time to journal in your notepad or Book of Shadows. I have created some rather humorous drawings of my shadow aspects in my Book of Shadows. This has helped me to not take myself too seriously when it comes to letting go of some of this old stuff. When I look at some of these entries I also realize how much I have transformed and grown through my Shadow Work.

AFFIRMATIONS

Words are powerful. Words express symbols, images, and concepts. The most powerful effect of your words can be to activate your energy, attract other helpful spirits or energies, and to direct these influences in a very specific way to target you're your desired outcome. Much like spell-work or incantations, affirmations are simply making a powerful statement of attainment.

If you have subjected yourself, knowingly or unknowingly to long periods of negative self-talk, positive affirmations are the most simple and magical antidote.

Negative, self-sabotaging thoughts are the food which fuel of our shadow parts. The messages which we give to ourselves are the most important and impactful messages we hear. Our internal dialogue determines our outlook and directs the course of our life.

If you are filled with a sarcastic, self-imposed, negative inner critic, it's time to pull the plug on this shadow remnant. Any ongoing negative commentary will slowly mutilate your creativity, your self-esteem, and your very soul.

You may have been raised in a household where you were criticized or shamed and as a result developed a self-deprecating dialogue. Your family may be responsible for what happened in the past, but you are responsible for what happens with you now. You can continue to live in the past, or you can change your thoughts and beliefs and set yourself free.

We have a choice in what we believe. What we choose to believe essentially forms our world. If we persist in believing ourselves to be victims, that is what we become. If we choose to believe we are open and deserving of love, acceptance, and expansion, we are. We will always have the choice. As we get used to directing our thoughts to a level of higher energy, our emotions and actions will naturally start to follow.

Affirmations are a way to rebuild. Use affirmations every day because their power will grow as the old walls of shame and criticism and old ways of thinking fall away. Like waking from a bad dream, affirmations wake up the aspects of you that have been blocked by shadows. As the shadow lifts we become more awake and aware of the choices we make every day.

There's a secret to boosting up the power of affirmations. The use of affirmations are more powerful while you are in a hypnagogic state (hypnagogic is the transitional state between wakefulness and sleep.) So while going to bed, just before falling asleep, use this time to visualize or use affirmations for increased impact.

You may want to start with one simple affirmation, such as: ***Today I choose to completely love and accept myself.***

Below are some basic affirmations you might find useful:

Today I will take action instead of reacting

Today I will listen to my intuitive self.

Today is a new day and I will let go of the past

Today I will be confident in my decisions

Today I will choose to see the positive

Today I am the creator of my own joy

Today I acknowledge and use my talents

Today I leave fear behind and go with the flow of life

Today I use good judgment and make decisions

Today my feelings inside match my outside

Today I let go of the past

Today I focus on what actions I can take here and now

Today I let go of my old expectations of others

Today I give myself permission to be me

Today I seek out healthy friendships

Today I no longer seek to manage the impressions others have of me

Today I am worthwhile, just as I am

Today my emotions enrich my life and spirit

Today I let go of yesterdays pain

Today I choose only positive actions that are best for me

Today I can be assertive

Today I am happy with myself

Today I can release my anger in healthy ways

Today I will be good to myself

Today I honor and accept myself

Today I surround myself with people who respect me and treat me well

Of course being a witch I often use spell-work, so I might take an affirmation and turn it into an incantation. This is highly effective as the rhyme and rhythm quiets the conscious part of your mind, making it easier to work subliminally on the subconscious. So instead I might use:

"All troubled conditions,
Old hurts and pain,
Burn away now
So that none remain."

*"Before me now is born a new day,
As opportunity and success pave the way,
I will walk the walk, with my feet on the ground,
And in all my affairs, with success, I'll be crowned."*

*"False expectations, now burn away
A new way of being, opens the way."*

Or

*"The realm of Shadow holds the key,
And now my spirit's flying free."*

You get the idea. Words are powerful! Choose the words that impact you the most profoundly. These can be simple affirmative statements, incantations, poem fragments, or meaningful quotes. Carefully choose the best words to create, or recreate, your most personal self-talk.

WINDOW TO THE SOUL

There is an ethereal channel, like a stream in which energy flows from your heart and out through your eyes. With your energy alone, you can communicate this stream of love, and channel it through your gaze. Use this energy to speak directly with your own soul.

Relax, take a couple of deep, cleansing breaths, and cast off any worries or concerns.

Gaze into the mirror and look upon your face. Allow no judgment. Look beyond the outer aspects of age, beauty, or other physical assessments that small mind is drawn to or repelled by.

See yourself through the eyes of a child, without judgment. See yourself as a child, the soul within who carries a spark of Divinity, and is always deserving of your love and respect.

Look deeply into your eyes. Allow what is held there to be mirrored back to you. What do you see? Is there pain or fatigue? Is there love or gratitude? Do you see a stranger or a friend?

Look deeply into your eyes and silently tell yourself as the soul within you, "I love and accept you."

See the Divine spark at the center of your being as it ignites and fills you up with light.

As you move through your day after this, allow that stream of energy to flow from your heart to your eyes as you interact compassionately with others. Allow the love and acceptance within to flow out of your eyes and into their soul.

SACRED ALTAR/ SHADOW RELEASE

Forgive yourself for accumulating these shadowy aspects of self. We all have them! Changing may be a little scary. You may find yourself later wanting to pull some of the discarded aspects back in. Try to examine the root of that particular shadow trait. If you have made a list of shadow aspects you might then lay it out on an altar before the Divine and asked that it be lifted from you.

A powerful way to do this is by burning one black candle (which you may want to dedicate to the deity, higher power, or other helpful spirit that you are working with) on your altar. Take your list of shadow aspects and burn it in the candle flame. See yourself being uplifted as the flame grows and the smoke rises. You might choose to recite this incantation:

"Heal this soul from dark of night,
In all places grown dark
There is now only light."

While watching the smoke rise, see any shadow aspects going upward to the Divine Source where it will be transformed into a more usable energy before it returns to cycle back into the flow of life.

DARK NIGHT OF THE SOUL

If you have felt that you have come into a space where life holds no hope and no meaning; that you are just going through the motions, or that it is sometimes just difficult to breathe as you are sucked further down into a black hole, you may be experiencing a "Dark Night of the Soul."

If a Dark Night sounds like some scary, f'ed up, shit, I'm here to let you know, yes it totally is! The Dark Night is reaching a point in your spiritual development where nothing works and things no longer make sense. The spiritual crises cannot be bargained with. All falsehoods have been stripped away. You no longer feel connected to the things and people which you used to find entertaining. Much of life seems pointless. You cannot drink it, drug it, or gamble it away. You may resort to more socially acceptable strategies, such as numbing yourself with sex, television, or food, but these offer no relief either.

The good news about the Dark Night is that is has a beginning, a middle, and an end. The place where it hurts the most is in the middle! Dark Nights often occur when a person has experienced deep spiritual growth and is in transition to a deeper understanding and awareness in their life. This painful transition often involves a painful letting go of former ideas, beliefs, and constructs which previously formed a large part of one's identity or ego. Core pieces of identity such as career, relationships, creative outlets, and belief systems, may be unraveled and lose all meaning.

You are at a spiritual crossroad. You may have already done a lot of shadow work and emotional healing but you are on the brink! Like the Fool in the tarot, you have one foot over the chasm, but it's so dark. Spirit is telling you that you have more work to do regarding ego. Your spirit guides, teachers, and allies are rooting for you and hoping that you progress through this dark night for they have so much to teach you. A higher spiritual force is working in your life but moving through the darkness is disorienting. You may feel like you are flailing around trying to grasp control of the uncontrollable. And you probably are. That's just it. What you need to do is let go, let the Dark Night flow.

The Dark Night of the Soul is a time of major transformation. Know that you are going through this for a reason and that you will come out the other side of it with a heightened awareness and understanding of your life. The more this transition is resisted, the longer it lasts. Much like the crux of Shadow Work, the more you resist the Dark Night, the more you resist the Shadow, the stronger they become and the longer they last. Work to transform your shadow, but don't beat yourself up with it. Face those hidden parts of self and you will transform

The process of the Dark Night can be likened to Shamanic "Descent to the Underworld," or Inanna's descent through the seven gates of the underworld. It is a painful and often confusing process and the Dark Night doesn't just last a night. Usually it lasts anywhere from a few weeks to a number of months. Any efforts to speed it up will likely make it last longer. The most important things are to not beat yourself up, to get out of your own way, and to just let it happen. You can't fight the storm, but you can sail the storm and come out safe and whole on the other side of it.

The spiritual paradox is that the Dark Night of the Soul is a gift from spirit. The gift is that you take a massive jump forward in spiritual development in a short amount of time, painful though it may be. And when you have truly embraced your Shadow and feel ready to move forward, you may want to work with or explore some truly transformative Dark Goddess energy to help you through the Dark Night.

DARK GODDESS ALCHEMY

If you already work with goddess energy, or are open to working with goddess energy, there are a number of dark goddess underworld deities which can be worked with in transformative shadow work.

Some of the dark goddesses (or a dark aspect of the goddess) which may be open to working with you are Aradia, Brigid, Kali, Hecate, Isis, Lilith, the Morrigan, Persephone, Sekhmet, Maat, and the sister goddesses of dark and light Inanna and Ereshkigal.

Before embarking on dark goddess work, you will need to study and become familiar with the goddess you are drawn to working with. You will also need to find out if this goddess will accept working with you. Many spirit workers find that the goddess will most often choose you rather than the other way around. At the very least you will need to go into meditation with the goddess you are drawn to, to ask and find out! Once you know the goddess which you are aligned with, and have found that she will work with you, then proceed to the dark goddess alchemical shadow work outlined below.

Items required for the work: a **black stone** such as Black Obsidian, Snowflake Obsidian, Black Jasper, Smokey Quartz, or Black Calcite (shaman's stone).

A simple **black candle** (optionally dressed with Shadow Oil or Dark Goddess Oil) dedicated to the goddess.

Shadow Oil

To a carrier oil of Fractionated Coconut Oil or Sweet Almond Oil add:
Bay Leaf Essential Oil- 7 drops
Clary Sage Essential Oil- 7 drops
Patchouli Essential Oil- 7 drops
Add: a bit of Solomon Seal Root and a bit of crumbled Sage leaves

Dark Goddess Oil

To a carrier oil of Fractionated Coconut Oil or Sweet Almond Oil add:
Cedarwood Essential Oil- 13 drops
Cinnamon Essential Oil – 7 drops
Myrrh Essential Oil – 3 drops
Add: a pinch of Crossroad Dirt and Sulfur

Have pen, paper, notepad, or Book of Shadows on hand to journal your experiences. Light your candle and position the stone or crystal in front of it.

Get into a comfortable sitting position with your feet on the floor. You want to be comfortable but alert. Set your intention. Gaze into the flame and the reflection of it on the stone in front of you.

Relax and take a few deep cleansing breaths. You are ready.

DARK GODDESS ELEMENTAL ALCHEMY:

Relax, close your eyes, and focus on your breathing.

Invite the Universal Energy to flow through you by entering your Crown Chakra and flowing downward through you and into the Earth.

This energy flows through you cleansing and balancing each cell of your body. The energy flows downward and out of your feet, connecting you to the Earth's energy.

Continue to focus on your breathing as you sense the energy rising, flowing upward and exiting through your Crown Chakra, connecting you to the Cosmic energy, strengthening your connection to the Divine, and awakening your inner vision.

See yourself entering the Void through the black stone or crystal. As you sink in, you sense yourself suddenly falling downward, rapidly passing through dirt, roots, and stones. As you fall through the earth, you start to feel cleansed of all ungrounded or unwanted energy and notice that you feel physically stronger and lighter. This fall continues until you come to a stop in the underworld of the inner planes.

You look through the mist to your left and see a river with many people on its bank, who appear to be either sleeping or waiting. To your right you see a series of caves and find that you are drawn to one of them. As you walk into the cave you become engulfed in darkness.

You continue to walk, carefully ahead through total darkness until you come upon gusts of powerful winds moving to and through your very being. These powerful winds are so strong that they are pushing you back and you have to focus on moving intently, one step at a time as you force your way through. The pervasive winds clear your mind, blowing away all negative thoughts, all negative self - talk, and all old ways of thinking which no longer serve you and you find that you are able to get through to the other side of these winds.

As you continue deeper, into the darkness of the cave, you come upon a curtain of fire which you know you must pass through to continue your journey. As you step into the curtain of fire, you hear the flames crackle and feel a resistance as you attempt to pass through to the other side. As you stand within the flames you realize all of your fears and self – doubt are now burning away and being replaced with the flame of your soul, your creative passionate self freely wells up within. The fragrance of sweet wood smoke fills your nostrils as you take a deep breath and notice that you are now able to step through to the other side and exit the curtain of fire. An excitement builds within you as you continue on through the darkness.

As you continue walking, you come upon a deep pool of cool water. As you walk out into the water, you feel the bottom slip away and find yourself sinking deeper and deeper into its depths. As you sink downward, you find that the healing energy of this water washes away all old anger, hurts, and sorrow. As you pass through the water, you begin to sense how these things that served and protected you in the past are now no longer needed and you feel relief as they now slip away.

You pass through and come out on the other side, below this body of water and into a cavern. As you look around you see there are many passageways leading away from this central location. You are drawn to one of the passageways which is lit up with torch lights, and walk through there.

You find that this passageway leads you to the ruins of an ancient temple. It is there, seated upon a black marble throne, you find the goddess you seek.

Take this time to commune with her. Leave her a gift, be respectful, and thank her for your alchemical journey.

When you are ready to return, you see the ceiling of the temple open up, and with a slight pull, feel yourself being pulled upward. You move back through the stones, roots, and dirt, until you find yourself drawn back into the room where you started.

Take this time to get a drink of water and write your experience down in your notepad, journal, or Book of Shadows. Continue to work with the goddess by developing a give and take relationship. Communicate with her and ask for help when struggling with shadow aspects. Always know that you can take this journey more than once. Light candles and incense to honor her and to thank her whenever she has helped you. Some of you may go even further into spirit work with the dark goddess. One effective way to do this might be by ensouling a statue or a picture of the goddess to act as a ward or doorway guardian to your home.

EXTERNAL WORK

Regarding self-esteem, one of the best ways to build it is by doing the next right thing. We will naturally feel good about ourselves when we do right by others. Actions speak louder than words. Getting right with everyone around you is basically clearing away any past wrongs and treating all that you come into contact with, with respect. You probably have a pretty good idea of which people you will have to make an effort with to right any past wrongs.

Don't beat yourself up. All that's required here is making an effort to set things right. If you owe someone money- figure out a way to pay them back. If you can't do it all at once- maybe give them a little each a month until it's paid in full. If you have spoken in anger- go to that person face to face and let them know that you are sorry for your part in any altercation.

One of the most important things to keep in mind is that you have no control over how people will react to you. The other person may not respond kindly. I believe you will find that most of the time people do respond favorably to your efforts. If they don't there is nothing that you can do about that. The important thing is to do your part to the best of your ability and let it go. "Letting go" also entails letting go of the other person's response to you. You've done what you can and now it's water under the dam. Always keep in mind that these simple acts will go a long way toward clearing away your unwanted shadow aspects.

True "letting go" is a spiritual paradox. By letting go you automatically call all of your power back into yourself and become complete.

If you have had any blockages in connecting to spirit, I think you'll find it much easier to connect after doing what you can to heal, transform, or let go of your shadow aspects. Working to transform your shadow really does work.

Keeping Yourself in Fit Spiritual Condition

Seek a Divine spiritual connection through joy not fear. Connection can often be found through nature, while doing things like watching a sunrise over the water, or taking time to gaze at the stars.

Talk to your higher power/s, higher self, or whatever your conception of deity or the Divine is. Do it throughout your day, just as you would talk to a dear friend.

Take some quiet time every day. Lose the technological barrage for ten minutes every morning as a way of taking time to meditate or listen. Spirit may be talking but we can easily be too bombarded in the material stream of life to "hear" anything.

A good reason to decrease your amount of online use is that social media breeds anonymity which acts as a powerful disinhibitor that taps into the worst aspects of human behavior.

Quit taking stock of other's faults and concentrate on improving yourself. Find out what positive actions you can pack into the stream of life.

Occasionally try to do something good for someone else without taking credit for it.

Find something to laugh about every day.

Make a gratitude list.

Don't compare your insides to other peoples' outsides.

Don't gossip or trash talk about others. Whenever you do that, you're actually feeding a shadow aspect of yourself. If you have issues with someone, talk **_to_ them** rather than talking **_about_ them**.

Choose to surround yourself with positive people. The positivity is contagious. (As is negativity- if you find yourself surrounded with negative people, you might want to evaluate what is going on.) According to author Mitch Horowitz, the number one way we get drained of personal power is by surrounding ourselves with people who don't support us.

Strive to make your life as balanced as possible. Exercise your body, eat healthy food, get the proper amount of sleep, don't engage in replaying old hurts, work to let go of or resolve emotional baggage, pray or talk to your Higher Power whatever that concept is for you- God, Goddess, Higher Power, Great Spirit, and then take time to listen through meditation.

Incorporate the forgiveness principle into your life. This is the concept that you become what you don't forgive. This can become a pattern which will sweep into your life. Acknowledge the pain and injustice but also forgive as a way to heal yourself.

Occasionally do a self assessment. What is it that takes up most of your thoughts or your feelings on a day to day basis? If you are filled with resentments, or old hurts, spirit might not be able to connect with you. There's no room left, you've let yourself become filled up with whatever it is that preoccupies all your inner energy. If it is something that is not enhancing your life, let it go. Just like a storeroom, you only have so much space inside to utilize. Don't fill it up with these sorts of things that hold you back. Clear off yesterdays goods from the shelf space in your mind. You'll soon feel lighter than air. It'll become much easier then to connect to spirit.

The more you take care of yourself, the better and more useful you will become to others, in the physical world and in the spirit world. The better shape that you are in and the more balanced you are, the less likely are you to encounter negative spirits or have yourself be open to spirit attachments. Keep yourself on a positive track.

Remember: Just as being surrounding with positive people in the physical world is a healthy choice, so it goes in the spirit world. One way to accomplish this is by the creation of an Ancestor Altar in your home. Not only is this a lovely way to honor your loved ones who have passed over, it is also a savvy way to create a naturally built in aura of protection for you and your family. (For more info on ancestor work, see Book Three: The Guide to Spirit Work). The reason it works this way is simple, it's because your ancestors on the other side of the veil love you, and want to watch over you.

CHAPTER NINE
SOUL RETRIEVAL

Soul Retrieval, (sometimes called Soul Recovery) has its roots within the practice of ancient shamanism and is the process of recovering a lost or missing piece of an individual's soul which had splintered off (usually due to a traumatic event) and then bringing the missing piece back to reunite with the rest of the soul as a way to heal and make it whole again. What was referred to as Soul Loss in the past, might today be referred to as the psychological term- dissociation.

The ancients believed that the loss of one's soul, or a part of it, caused illness to manifest. The shaman would then journey to the place where the soul, or the fragment, had departed and then bring the missing part back to the ill person to reintegrate and restore their health by making them whole again. Depending on the culture and beliefs of the tribe, the shaman's journey may have taken him or her to the astral plane, the underworld, to the past, or to different dimensions. Once there, the shaman would usually do whatever it took to bring it back; this might entail singing it back, talking it back, tricking it back, or even trapping and dragging it back.

Soul Retrieval is a term used to indicate the locating and returning of a fragment of the Self that splintered off during a time of trauma; although this "missing piece", or "missing pieces" are still energetically attached to the individual, it is a part disconnected from the consciousness of the self and needs to be reintegrated into the whole.

Soul Fragmentation is a survival mechanism and is sometimes referred to as compartmentalization or dissociation. It often occurs swiftly and spontaneously as a way to survive a traumatic event and protect the integrity of the rest of the Soul. When this happens an individual may section off the physical, mental, and emotional reactions during a time of extreme stress. This sectioned-off part of self is often left behind as a way for the person to keep functioning by minimizing or escaping the painful aspects of a situation. This sectioning off of self will create a void or empty space.

Remember that anytime a void is created within your spirit, soul, or energetic bodies, it will seek to be filled. Any form of soul loss, leaves a person with the feeling of not being whole, or feeling that a part of them are missing. If left to chance, this void often ends up being filled with psychic debris, or in a worst case scenario it could be filled with a spirit attachment. This psychic debris may often take the form of spiritual, emotional, or mental numbing and dissociation, through such things as alcohol, drug abuse, sexual addictions, dysfunctional relationship patterns, and obsession with food, work, or any other compulsion. This often leads to emotional distress, a weakened immune system, and may eventually breaks down to physical illness.

The concept of Soul Retrieval may resonate for many of us. How often have we heard related phrases or concepts in everyday life? People will sometimes say things like they feel like "a part of them is missing," or refer to someone having a "hole in their soul." Most of us have experienced some Soul Loss somewhere along our journey through life, although not everybody needs a Soul Retrieval. It usually depends on the amount of impact the event had on an individual.

It's interesting to note that the word shaman means "one who sees in the dark" and the term comes to us from the ancient Tungus tribe in Siberia. In our modern age, many of us struggle to "see in the dark." The noise, speed, and busy-ness all around us often interferes with the process of spiritual development or being able to see with our "spirit eyes."

To operate in the physical realm, we are (for the most part) contained within the walls of our five senses. Each of our senses: sight, touch, hearing, smell, and taste, makes up a wall. These walls are our filters which help us to live in the physical realm. They function as filters to let in the information we need and filter out the extraneous information. One example of this is the color spectrum. We can see the light waves that make up a rainbow of color ranges. We can see red, orange, yellow, green, blue, indigo, violet, and so on, but we know that there are colors above and below this spectrum of color which we are unable to see. Other factors which act as filters to reality are the intellect and conditioning. One way to operate in the nonphysical realm is to get outside of these walls or filters and to "see in the dark" by journeying or visioning.

As a Reiki practitioner and shamanic witch, many of the simple techniques I use are adaptations that have worked for me over the years and incorporate aspects of magic, shamanism, Reiki, and other forms of energy healing. The methods I use and teach do not involve the use of drumming or any psychoactive substances. I begin the journey of Soul Retrieval in the same place where I start all of my journeys, which is within the spiritual nexus of the Void.

In your journeys you may invite spirit guides or power animals to accompany you, they may appear spontaneously, or you may go it alone. Power animals that spontaneously appear along the way are usually there to lend the magical assistance of their powers in locating the lost, providing protection, or aiding healing. I've gone solo in many journeys but have also experienced a variety of spirit animals in the form of a shape-shifting dog/ wolf, a dove, and a great crane. The dog power animal for me acts much like a tracking dog in locating the lost and shifts into the form of a wolf when protection is needed. Sometimes I am able to see or sense through the "eyes" of this spirit. The dove and crane are also both very protective and healing and have appeared to me as the soul fragment reunites with the whole or during other healing processes.

The method described here for Soul Retrieval is simple and is much like the other practices in this book. It can be used as way of healing yourself or to guide another person through the process as a way to heal by recovering the lost parts of self. Before attempting Soul Retrieval, it is necessary for the trauma or root cause to be identified first.

Soul Splintering or Separation

It is believed that each of our souls arrives into this current life whole. Due to traumatic events, or emotions that are unprocessed, a part of, or all of your soul may separate from the whole. Soul splintering or separation is very often a survival or escape mechanism. Some of the events that are possible causes of soul loss or separation could be:

Loss of a loved one through death or divorce
Experiencing childhood physical, sexual, or emotional abuse
Experiencing any form of abuse as an adult (especially from someone you had previously trusted)

Physical trauma, like: surgery, being in a car accident, being assaulted
Former Military with Post Traumatic Stress Disorder
Surviving catastrophic events
Alcohol or Drug Addiction
Severe physical illnesses
Experiencing deep betrayal
Loss of job or business
Witnessing acts of violence
Witnessing catastrophic accidents or events

Soul loss is possible anytime there is an experience that is either so sudden, or so traumatic, that the person is unable to fully digest, or accept it. The shock of it causes dissociation and the individual may section off the physical, mental, and emotional reactions. This part of self gets left behind and becomes lost. Some people who have undergone Soul Retrieval report that the lost part of self takes the appearance of the individual at the age they were when the trauma took place and this is also what I experienced on my journeys. Soul fragments can be found at the time and place of the traumatic event and requires accessing the Akashic records.

Not many of us are able to journey through life unscathed. It is possible to have some soul fragmentation with little or no problems resulting from it. Sometimes the soul splinters, or fragments minute amounts and it causes no problems in our daily functioning. Sometimes traumatic events make us stronger. Soul Retrieval is not necessary for everyone. Soul Retrieval is meant for those who have repeated, or persistent problems that are able to be traced back to a traumatic experience that occurred earlier in their lives.

Some of the Symptoms of possible Soul Loss are:

Chronic feelings of sadness, melancholia, and depression
Chronic sleep disorders; too much or too little
Chronic sickness
Immune deficiency disorders
Feeling empty
Feeling numb
Frozen feelings
Feeling "stuck" and unable to move forward in life
Addiction problems
Post Traumatic Stress
Adult or childhood memory gaps
Chronic unresolved anger
Chronic fear
Chronic unresolved grief
Chronic pain
Eyes with the look of "nobody home"

Even if you have never experienced any soul separation or loss, I recommend journeying to the Pool of Memories yourself to experience it firsthand before guiding someone else there. The Pool of Memories also leads to many other areas that you might later want to explore. The Akashic Records which holds life memories is just one place within the vast and powerful Pool of Memories. The other places located within the Pool contain much, much more, such as the realm which contains all possible magical and mystical knowledge or another realm within the pool which holds all the secrets of nature.

Guidelines in Preparing for Soul Retrieval

Before beginning, you need to identify the past traumatic event where you believed the soul fragmentation occurred.

Receiving a key awareness sometime during the process is vital and acts as a catalyst for reintegrating the lost piece of self back into the whole. Receiving this personal awareness is not complicated it simply means gaining an understanding or perspective about the event which caused the soul to fragment. The cause might be linked to hurt, fear, protection, grief, or other psychic wounding. This awareness is different for everyone and will be highly individual.

With proper preparation the Soul Retrieval will go as planned. Occasionally it may not for a couple of different reasons. One reason may be that the person thought that they had experienced soul separation but upon entering the memory find that they did not. If this is the case, no harm will be experienced from journeying to the Akashic Records, just stop the process and return.

Another reason the Soul Retrieval may need to be stopped is if you, or the person being guided is having too difficult of a time to remain with the memory long enough to complete the process due to retraumatization. It is always okay to stop and try again in the future.

You may journey alone or with a Power Animal or Spirit Guide.

Another important thing to know is that there is no "one and done" for multiple issues of soul fragmentation. If you find that you have several past events that may have caused soul loss, please realize that a *separate or individual* journey will need to be done for each event. To give a proper amount of rest time between each Soul Retrieval journey, you should wait a period of one to two months before doing the next one. It usually takes approximately three to six weeks to cycle through complete reintegration and healing of body, mind, and spirit.

The technique I describe here is one that can be done on yourself or you may guide another person through it. Set aside at least thirty minutes of undisturbed time.

During the Soul Retrieval you will journey through that spark of Divinity known as the Spiritual Nexus then and into the Pool of Memories. You will revisit the event that caused your soul to separate, receive a key awareness into why the soul separated, retrieve the lost piece of your soul, and bring this missing piece back to yourself. Receiving the key awareness is vital and acts as a catalyst for reintegrating the lost piece of self back into the whole. Receiving this awareness is not complicated as it simply means gaining an understanding of the event that caused the soul fragmentation. Once you have returned ground and center your energy, and then record your experience.

Examples of Key Insights might be:

Death of a loved one/ overwhelming grief

Experiencing any form of abuse/ fear, protection, emotional numbing, grief, toxic shame

Deep loss or abandonment

Witnessing a catastrophic event/ fear, survivor guilt

Alcohol or Drug Addiction/ fear, frozen feelings, toxic shame

I kept the above examples very brief as there could never be an effective simple listing for these sorts of complex issues. I placed these examples here simply to provide a general idea of what a trauma related key insight might be. Many are fear-based or are rooted in deep anguish or grief. While doing my own soul retrieval, I stated, "I am going to locate the memory of when my friend died." The act of doing my own soul retrieval triggered the insight which put me in touch with the core feelings of abandonment and grief that I had denied myself at the time which triggered some soul fragmentation.

KEY STEPS TO SOUL RETRIEVAL:

Identify the event which triggered the Soul Loss
Set your intention to access the time and place of that event
Get into a relaxed state
Channel the Universal Energy
Enter the Void
Sink into the Pool of Memories
Access the time and place of the event within the Akashic Records
Receive key awareness
Bring the missing piece of your soul back
As you journey back through the Pool of Memories the missing part of the soul merges with the whole

Cleanse and clear the room or area where you will be working with Sage, Palo Santo, or a cleansing incense combination that you've created (see Chapter Five) and visualize the area filling with a protective white light.

Ready to Begin:

Get into a comfortable sitting position with your feet on the floor. You want to be comfortable but alert. Set your intention by stating silently or out loud the past triggering experience you are going to access. One way might be to state "I am going now to locate the memory of (event)."

Relax and take a few deep cleansing breaths.

Previously to access the Void we used an element, such as a stone or a candle flame to connect to connect with a spark of the Divine. In this example we will connect to the spark of the Divine within ourselves to enter the Void.

Soul Retrieval:

Relax, close your eyes, and focus on your breathing.

Invite the Universal Energy to flow through you by entering your Crown Chakra and flowing downward into the Earth.

This energy flows through you cleansing and balancing each cell of your body. The energy flows downward and out of your feet, connecting you to the Earth's energy.

Continue to focus on your breathing as you sense the energy rising, flowing upward and exiting through your Crown Chakra, connecting you to the Cosmic energy, strengthening your connection to the Divine, and awakening your inner vision.

Now be mindful of the regular rhythm of your breath and slowly, one breath at a time, focus on the center of your being.

One breath at a time, move your mind to where you perceive the center of your being is, and find the core of your being.

See within you, where your soul is housed and allow your mind to connect within the center of your being.

Allow yourself to touch that spark of Divinity and ignite the flame of your soul.

Now with each outward breath, visualize this light expanding.

With each outward breath, visualize this light getting stronger.

With each outward breath visualize this light filling your entire being.

With your mind at the very center of that light, know that this light, this power, contains all that you are. Know that this power contains all that you have been, and know that this power contains the potential of all you are yet to become.

Continue to focus on your breathing as you allow this light to expand out beyond your body.

With each breath you take, see this light expand out further and into the room.

In your mind's eye this light fills the room in front of you, top to bottom, and side to side.

See this light move, almost dancing as it swirls into the shape of a vortex before you.

This vortex is a passage way, a tunnel of spiraling light that leads to into the Void, a gateway to the inner realms.

Now see yourself standing up and walking into the middle of this vortex where you feel a slight pull before you exit out on the other side.

Everything else drifts away until you find yourself completely within this space of nothingness.

The Void is a place that serves as the Axis and Axle of all possible realms; this spiritual nexus is limitless and ever expanding.

You begin to walk and find yourself moving along a grassless path. This path takes you along the edge of an old-growth forest.

You keep walking until you come upon a smooth, clear lake reflecting all that is above it.

This lake is the Pool of Memories. You find that you are able to walk out on the lake, on top of the water, and when you come directly to the center of it, you find yourself sinking downward, into the water.

As you continue to sink down deeper and deeper, you realize that this water doesn't affect your ability to breathe, it nourishes you.

You continue to sink down deeper, until you find yourself beneath this body of water where you now enter the Hall of Memories holding the Akashic Records.

You see ahead of you and all around you, flowing, undulating walls expanding outwards in all directions and flowing to infinity. These walls hold shelves upon shelves of countless books and these books contain a multitude of fragments of light.

This library holds the records of all human thoughts, actions, emotions, and memories.

On a shelf before you at eye level, you see a book with your name on it. This book contains the record of your soul.

Take the book down from the shelf and intuitively open it to a random spot. This page contains the time and place where your soul fragmented and serves as a window to your soul.

This page is an actual window through which you can view the time, place, and memory that you seek.

When you are ready to continue, look through this window where you will immediately see and recognize yourself as you were at the age and time of the memory. This image of yourself symbolizes your Soul Fragment. Continue to watch as you see the memory play out. What you see may take the form of a movie or a series of images playing out before your eyes. You may see symbols, or colors which take on significance. You may hear a message, a word or a sound, or you may just gain an inner sense of knowing.

Ask that you receive the key awareness, information, or insight that you need at this time. How this manifests is highly personal and different for everyone. Allow your intuition to guide you to the hidden space between you and the part of yourself that fragmented. This space may hold fear, grief, or other hidden aspects, and contains an understanding on why your soul fragmented.

Take as much time as you need for this to occur. Remember that you cannot proceed to the next action until you acquire this key insight. This key is necessary as it is needed to open the door.

(Pause at this juncture for as long as needed to complete this step.)

Now that you have obtained this necessary insight, the lost fragment of your soul needs to be to be retrieved.

A door appears before you. This is a door you will be able to step through and walk into your memory. The lost fragment of your soul that you came to retrieve waits inside.

It is time to enter your memory by entering the door. When you feel ready place the book back on the shelf, open the door, and walk in.

You see your soul fragment there which appears as you did at the time of this memory.

Do what feels right to you at this time. There might be something you want to say to this lost part of you, you may want to hug or embrace this part of your soul, or you may just want to welcome it back.

This piece of your soul knows where it belongs. Your soul fragment will instinctively recognize you and will always come with you freely and spontaneously.

Take the hand of the soul fragment and lead this part of yourself back out the door, making sure you close the door as you exit.

Hold the Soul Fragment's hand and set your intention to return as you begin your journey back.

See yourself and the Soul Fragment move upward and exit this realm through the same entryway. As you float back up through the Pool of Memories the soul fragment spontaneously merges with the rest of your soul.

You walk along the path after this and quickly find the vortex located there.

As you enter the vortex you feel a sudden pull, and promptly find yourself back in your physical body.

See any portals or passageways that you may have opened now closing.

Take a deep, cleansing breath and when you feel ready, wiggle your fingers and toes, and open your eyes.

Take the time to ground yourself, clear any psychic debris, and drink some water before journaling your experiences. If you were guiding another person through Soul Retrieval, advise them to do the same.

CHAPTER TEN
EXPLORING & HEALING PAST LIVES

At some point in your spirit work you may come across an individual who has psychic debris or other unexplained issues cropping up in life (such as- relationship problems, chronic pain, irrational fears, a feeling of being blocked or stuck, and unable to move forward in life). The key word here is *unexplained*. Unlike Soul Retrieval, where you are able to trace the cause of soul separation to a traumatic event, you will often find that your biggest clue to a possible past life influence are issues which have no explanation. In other words, you will not be able to trace the "symptoms" to any cause in this lifetime.

Upon investigation you may find clues that point toward a traumatic event in a past life. Some spirit workers and energy healers refer to this event as a "Past Life Root Event" or a "Past Life Karmic Trigger." I usually refer to the past life cause as a ***Past Life Cause-Effect***.

Strong emotions carry a charge, similar to an electrical charge. It is believed that a significant Past Life Cause-Effect can generate a powerful emotional charge which if not released might carry forward into the current lifetime.

Note how this has a similar cause and dynamic in relation to Soul Retrieval. The difference is in Soul Retrieval you are accessing a lost part of self triggered by a traumatic event which occurred in your current life time; in the healing of a Past Life Cause-Effect, the event occurred in a past life. The healing dynamic is similar in both Soul Retrieval and Past Life Healing, in that it is the insight gained about the traumatic events (current life or past life) on your journey that provides the healing to the individual.

Past Life Cause-Effects could potentially be caused by traumatic events, such as heart-break, a terrible deed or decision, catastrophic loss, or sudden or unexpected death in a past life by fire, drowning, fighting, a fatal fall, murder, accidental suicide, motor vehicle accident, or any of a countless number of other tragic scenarios. Whatever the cause, it most likely happened in a sudden and unexpected way, resulting in the person not being able to process the emotions it caused and consequently not being able to understand what happened.

Another cause might be traced back to a Karmic Debt incurred during a past lifetime. One way to look at this is related to the belief that we incarnate each lifetime to learn certain lessons while living in this plane of existence. Keeping in line with this way of thinking, a Karmic Debt may occur if we didn't learn the necessary lessons in the past life. A powerful emotional charged linked to an event in a past life is then carried over into this current lifetime. You would think that many of us may have racked up quite a few Past Life Cause Effects or Karmic Debts! Fortunately only one Past Life Cause -Effect will carry over into your current life from past lifetimes.

A **Past Life Intrusion** is when the effect of a traumatic event or a psychic cord/ bond from a past life spills over into the present day life. One example of a past life intrusion happened with me in my early thirties. For nearly a year I kept experiencing the feeling of a sudden fall and traumatic impact as if hitting something at a high rate of speed. At first it only happened while I was on the edge of sleep before becoming completely awake. As time went on, it began to happen at various times while wide awake throughout the day along with a couple of episodes of powerful Déjà vu. Upon doing a Past Life Healing session, I found the Past Life Cause-Effect was related to being a soldier/ warrior in a past life. During my past life journey to the cause effect, I very clearly saw myself in battle and hurled over a wall to my death. Seeing the cause effect through this event immediately illuminated a direct insight into what I had been experiencing. I am happy to report that afterwards I no longer experienced anymore of this unsettling sensation!

Possible Clues to Past Life/ aka Past Life Intrusions

An individual that experiences a strong and recurring sense of Déjà vu

Experiencing a deep sense of affiliation or closeness to a person or a set of people that are unrelated to you

Experiencing a strong aversion to a person or a set of people that you have no experience with

A profound feeling of affiliation or aversion to a formal group (such as a religious or political group) that you have had no experiences with

Feeling drawn to certain places in the world that you would like to visit

Feeling a unwarranted fear of visiting certain places in the world

Having recurrent dreams or nightmares of being familiar with unknown people or places

Having unusual memories that no one else in your family has

Having some knowledge, natural abilities, or talents that are strikingly different than what runs in your family

Having a strong passion in the realm of creativity, such as with art, or painting

Having issues with unwarranted fears, phobias, emotional issues, or chronic physical health problems for no apparent reason

Experiencing unexplained sensations

Experiencing unexplained pain

Having an intense fascination with specific segments of history

Some believe being born with birthmarks to be a physical sign of a past life

The good news is that a Past Life Healing Session can facilitate the release of this negative emotional charge and thus clear up Past Life Cause Effect problems. The following technique for past life journeying can be done on yourself or on another person.

KEY STEPS TO PAST LIFE HEALING:

Set your intention to access the time and place of the Past Life Cause Effect

Get into a relaxed state
Channel the Universal Energy
Enter the Inner Realms through the Void
Sink into the Pool of Memories
Walk the Hall of Past Lives
Access the time and place of the Past Life Cause Effect
Receive your key awareness
Past Life Healing begins
Journey back through the Pool of Memories

PREPARATION

Begin by preparing your environment. Decrease any external stimuli: turn off the cell phones, close the shades, and put the "do not disturb" sign on the door. Let others know not to disturb you during this time. Cleanse and clear the room you are working in by smudging with sage or sweet-grass beforehand as you visualize the room filling with clear golden-white light energy. If you feel like it, light a candle and burn a bit of meditation inducing incense such as sandalwood.

Dress in comfortable clothing and plan on spending 30 to 60 minutes to complete this process.

Place some drinking water, a pen, and your notebook or journal nearby.

If you are doing this for another person, take your time, talk about the process and see if they have any questions for you.

You or the person that you are doing this for should be seated in a comfortable chair. If it aids the relaxation process, quietly play some meditation music or ambient sound in the background.

If you are doing this for another person you may just read through, or adapt, the following guided meditation. If you are doing this for yourself, it is helpful to record yourself going through the guided meditation and then play it back to yourself when you are ready to go through and process it.

Get relaxed and begin with the intention of accessing the memory of the Past Life Cause-Effect. Visualize a powerful grid of protective layers of light surrounding you. You may ask that a Spirit Guide, Guardian Angel, or other helpful Spirit Allies be with you during this process, or you might prefer to go alone.

Cleanse and clear the room or area where you will be working with Sage, Palo Santo, or a cleansing incense combination that you've created (see Chapter Five) and visualize the area filling with a protective white light.

Ready to Begin:

Get into a comfortable sitting position with your feet on the floor. You want to be comfortable but alert. Set your intention to access the time and place of the Past Life Cause-Effect.

Previously to access the Void we used an element, such as a stone or a candle flame to connect to connect with a spark of the Divine. In this example we will connect to the spark of the Divine within ourselves to enter the Void.

PAST LIFE HEALING JOURNEY:

Relax, close your eyes, and focus on your breathing.

Breathe in to a count of four, and breathe out to a count of four. Take three or four deep, cleansing breaths.

As you breathe, give your head, heart, body, and soul permission to relax.
Cast off all tension and stress and as you breathe in, sense that you are drawing in love and peace. As you breathe out, sense all stress and tension flowing out,

Take another deep breath and invite the source of Universal Energy to flow through you.

See waves of light flowing down from its Source and entering the top of your head through the Crown Chakra.

Feel the waves of light flowing downward from your head to your toes, cleansing and balancing each cell of your body, and filling your entire being.

Continue to focus on your breathing, breathe in, and breathe out. See or sense these waves of light flowing downward and out through the bottom of your feet, and flowing down, down, downward- deep into the earth where this energy is transformed into clear and balance energy.

Now these light waves flow back upward, up, up, up, until it flows out through the Crown Chakra at the top of your head, continuing to flow upward and connecting you to the source of Spirit.

Continue to breathe deeply, in and out. You are now in the spirit space of connection between the earth's energy and the cosmic energy. Take another deep breath, in and out. Know that you are now opening up to the inner realms of spirit.

Now be mindful of the regular rhythm of your breath and slowly, one breath at a time, focus on the center of your being.

One breath at a time, move your mind to where you perceive the center of your being is, and find the core of your being.

See within you, where your soul is housed and allow your mind to connect within the center of your being.

Allow yourself to touch that spark of Divinity and ignite the flame of your soul.

Now with each outward breath, visualize this light expanding.

With each outward breath, visualize this light getting stronger.

With each outward breath visualize this light filling your entire being.

With your mind at the very center of that light, know that this light, this power, contains all that you are. Know that this power contains all that you have been, and know that this power contains the potential of all you are yet to become.

Continue to focus on your breathing as you allow this light to expand out beyond your body.

With each breath you take, see this light expand out further and into the room.

In your mind's eye this light fills the room in front of you, top to bottom, and side to side.

See this light move, almost dancing as it swirls into the shape of a vortex before you.

This vortex is a passage way, a tunnel of spiraling light that leads to into the Void, a gateway to the inner realms.

Now see yourself standing up and walking into the middle of this vortex where you feel a slight pull before you exit out on the other side.

Everything else drifts away until you find yourself completely within this space of nothingness.

The Void is a place that serves as the Axis and Axle of all possible realms; this spiritual nexus is limitless and ever expanding.

You begin to walk and find yourself moving along a grassless path. This path takes you along the edge of an old-growth forest.

You keep walking until you come upon a smooth, clear lake reflecting all that is above it.

This lake is the Pool of Memories. You find that you are able to walk out on the lake, on top of the water, and when you come directly to the center of it, you find yourself sinking downward, into the water.

As you continue to sink down deeper and deeper, you realize that this water doesn't affect your ability to breathe, it nourishes you.

You continue to sink down deeper, until you find yourself beneath this body of water where you now enter the Hall of Memories. Standing at the center of this great hall, you see ahead of you and all around you many other halls extending outward from this central one, their many flowing, undulating walls expanding outwards in all directions and flowing to infinity.

You find that one of the halls is illuminated brighter than all of the others and you find yourself drawn there. You begin to walk down this hall until you come upon the glow of a single, clear window on the wall before you.

This window to your soul holds the Cause-Effect memory of your past life that you came to see. Set your intention to receive any necessary key insight or understanding as you look at this past life memory.

When you feel ready, walk over to the window and look in.

As you look through this window you may see another person which you immediately recognize as yourself. Continue to watch as you see the memory play out. What you see may take the form of a movie or a series of images playing out before your eyes. You may see symbols, or colors which take on significance. You may hear a message, a word or a sound, or you may just gain an inner sense of knowing. Or you might only see your past life memory in the form of one image or symbol representing the Cause-Effect. Any of these are okay.

While viewing this memory, ask that you receive the key awareness, information, or insight that you need at this time.

(Pause at this juncture for as long as needed to complete this step.)

An understanding of the circumstances which caused the emotional charge connected to this event comes about quickly. Your understanding instantly triggers the release of the powerful, emotional charge linked to this past life memory and it will no longer create an intrusion or hold unwanted influence in your present life.

Return to the center of the great hall and feel yourself drawn upward, through the Pool of Memories. Walk back to the vortex where you entered the Void, and step back into it. As you enter the vortex, you will feel a sudden pull and find yourself back within your physical body.

See any portals or passageways that you may have opened, now closing.

Take a deep, cleansing breath and when you feel ready, wriggle your fingers and toes and open your eyes.

Your journey is complete.

Take the time to ground yourself, clear any psychic debris, and drink some water before journaling your experiences. If you were guiding another person through Past Life Healing, advise them to do the same.

CHAPTER ELEVEN
IN CLOSING

Before delving deeper into the spirit work practices outlined in Book Three, I wanted to address how to heal and maintain a healthy body, mind, and spirit. The path of the spirit worker, whether you are a witch, shaman, energy worker, magician, or otherwise can be filled with thorny conditions which can quickly deplete your energy if you are not prepared for it.

Choosing to be a walker between worlds often means either working with, or dealing with, shadows (your own or that of another person), spirits, and major energetic shifts. It is my hope that I have provided you with some useful information or insights that you can use as you navigate your way here in the physical realm or beyond the veil.

Much of this book is about reclaiming your own power, because the best way to work with spirit is by coming from a well of your own personal strength. Healing and transformation can be ugly, messy, painful, and also exciting! And it will most often lead you to places you never thought possible in the physical realm and beyond.

Like the ancient underworld goddess, we will sometimes have to make the descent into the shadow realms to truly understand ourselves and be transformed. As higher levels of understanding unfold, you open yourself up for the universe to line things up in ways that exceed even your best laid plans.

If my life had transpired only according to all of my best plans, I would have sold myself so short! Some of the practices in this book require you to keep walking forward in the dark, truly requiring a leap of faith. It is in the dark that you truly unlock the deepest mysteries.

My last word is to keep moving forward, even in the darkest night. I'll meet you on the other end.

Bibliography

Andrews, Ted. How to Meet and Work with Spirit Guides St. Paul, Minnesota: Llewellyn Publications, 1995

Allen, Sue. Spirit Releasement: A Practical Handbook. Winchester, UK Washington, USA: Books, 2007

Allen, Thomas B. Possessed: The True Story of an Exorcism. Lincoln, NE: iUniverse, 1994, 2000

Alvarado, Denise, and Angelique, Madrina. Working in 'da Boneyard. United States: Creole Moon Publications, 2012

Arana, Esmeralda. The Path: A Practical Approach To Sorcery. Lincoln, NE: Writer's Showcase, an imprint of iUniverse, Inc., 2002

Armand, Khi. Deliverance! Hoodoo Spells of Uncrossing, Healing, and Protection. Forestville, CA: Missionary Independent Spiritual Church, 2015, 2017

Ashour, Mustafa. The Jinn in the Qur'an and the Sunna. Dar Al Taqwa Ltd, 1989

Baglio, Matt. The Rite: The Making of a Modern Exorcist. New York, NY: Doubleday, a division of Random House, 2009

Baldwin, William J., Phd. Spirit Releasement Therapy: A Technique Manual
Terra Alta, WV: Headline Books, 2009

Ballabene, Alfred. (Translated by Corra) Thought Forms and Psychogons (about studies and practices with psychogons). Munich: BookRix GmbH & Co. KG, 2017

Balswin, William J, Phd. Healing Lost Souls: Releasing Unwanted Spirits From Your Energy Body. Charlottesville, VA: Hampton Roads Publishing Company, Inc, 2003

Johannes Trithemius: The Art of Drawing Spirits into Crystals. First English Ed. 1801 by Francis Barrett. New Edition 2016 Edited by Tarl Warwick

Baumann Brunke, Dawn. Animal Voices, Animal Guides: Discover Your Deeper Self through Communication with Animals. Rochester, Vermont: Bear & Company, 2004, 2009

Bean, Bill. Stranger than Fiction: True Supernatural Encounters of a Spiritual Warrior. Independently Published, 2018

Bellanger, Michelle. The Dictionary of Demons: Names of the Damned. Woodbury, Minnesota: Llewellyn Publications, 2012

Berry, Itzhak. Shamanic Transformations: True Stories of the Moment of Awakening. Rochester, Vermont: Destiny Books, 2015

Beyerl, Paul. The Master Book of Herbalism. Custer, Washington: Phoenix Publishing, Inc., 1984

Bohak, Gideon. Ancient Jewish Magic. Cambridge University Press, 2008

Braud, William, Phd. Distant Mental Influence: Its Contributions to Science, Healing, and Human Interactions. Charlottesville, VA: Hampton Roads Publishing Company, Inc., 2003

Briggs, Katharine. An Encyclopedia of Fairies: Hobgoblins, Brownies, Bogies, & Other Supernatural Creatures. Pantheon Books, 1978

Brother ADA. Ritual Magic For Conservative Christians. Columbus, Ohio: Thavma Publications, 2005, 2016

Buckland, Raymond. Solitary Séance: How You Can Talk with Spirits on Your Own.

Woodbury, MN: Llewellyn Publications, 2011

Budge, E. A. Wallis, Sir. Amulets And Superstitions. Dover Publications. 2011.

Cannon Reed, Ellen. The Witches Qabala: The Pagan Path and the Tree of Life. York Beach, ME: Red Wheel / Weiser, LLC, 1997

Carter, Chris. Science and Psychic Phenomena: The Fall of the House of Sceptics. Rochester, Vermont/ Toronto, Canada: Inner Traditions, 2012

Clarkson, Michael. Poltergeists: Examining Mysteries of the Paranormal. Buffalo, New York: Firefly Books, 2005

Coleman, Martin. Communing with the Spirits. York Beach, Maine: Samuel Weiser, Inc., 1998

Conway, D. J. Crystal Enchantments: A Complete Guide to Stones and Their Magical Properties. Crossing Press, 2000

Cowan, Tom. The Book of Séance: How to Reach Out to the Next World
Chicago: Contemporary Books, 1994

Crowfoot, Greg. A Sorcerer's Book of Art. Temple Island Press, 2007

Cumont, Franz Valery Marie. Afterlife in Roman Paganism, Dover Publications, 1959

Cunningham, Scott. Encyclopedia of Magical Herbs. Woodbury, Minnesota: Llewellyn Worldwide, 2007

Dale, Cyndi. The Complete Book of Chakra Healing, 2nd Ed., Woodbury, Minnesota: Llewellyn Publications, 1996, 2009, 2013.

Davidson, Gustav. A Dictionary of Angels: including the fallen angels. New York, NY: The Free Press, a division of Macmillan Inc., 1967, 1971

Davidson, Wilma. Spirit Rescue: A Simple Guide to Talking with Ghosts and Freeing Earthbound Spirits. Woodbury, Minnesota: Llewellyn Publications, 2007

Drury, Nevill. Don Juan, Mescalito And Modern Magic: The Mythology of Inner Space. London, England: Published by the Penguin Group, 1978, 1985

Drury, Neville. The Shaman And The Magician: Journeys Between The Worlds. England: Arkana, Penguin Group, 1987

DuQuette, Lon Milo. Angels, Demons, & Gods of the New Millennium, Musings on Modern Magick. York Beach, ME: Samuel Weiser, Inc., 1997

DuQuette, Lon Milo. Enochian Vision Magick. San Francisco, CA: Red Wheel/ Weiser, LLC. 2008

DuQuette, Lon Milo. Low Magick, It's All In Your Head . . . You Just Have No Idea How Big Your Head Is. Woodbury, Minnesota: Llewellyn Worldwide, 2017

Eno, Paul and Eno, Benjamin. Behind the Paranormal: Everything You Know Is Wrong. Atglen, PA: Schiffer Publishing, 2016

Evans, Darren and Guiley, Rosemary Ellen. The Zozo Phenomenon. New Milford, Connecticut: Visionary Living. Inc., 2016

Evans-Wentz, W.Y. Fairy Faith in Celtic Countries. New Age Edition, 2004 (first published in 1903)

Farmer, Dr. Steven D. Healing Ancestral Karma. San Antonio, TX: Hierophant Publishing, 2014

Fiore, Edith, Dr. The Unquiet Dead: A Psychologist Treats Spirit Possession. New York, NY: Ballantine Books a division of Random House, 1987

Foor, Daniel, Ph.D. Ancestral Medicine: Rituals for Personal and Family Healing. Rochester, Vermnont: Bear & Company, 2017

Fortune, Dion. Mystical Qabalah. Aquarian Press, 1987

Fortune, Dion. Psychic Self-Defense. York Beach, ME: Samuel Weiser, Inc. 1992, 1997

Gamache, Henri. The Master Book of Candle Burning. Plainview, NY: Original Publications, 1984

Goodwyn, Melba. Ghost Worlds: A Guide to Poltergeists, Portals, Ecto-Mist, & Spirit Behavior. Woodbury, Minnesota: Llewellyn Publications, 2007

Greer, John Michael. Encyclopedia of Natural Magic. Woodbury, Minnesota: Llewellyn Publications, 2005

Guiley, Rosemary Ellen. Demons & Demonology. Visionary Living, Inc., 2009

Guiley, Rosemary Ellen. The Encyclopedia of Ghosts and Spirits, 3rd Ed., New York, NY: Checkmark Books, 2007

Guiley, Rosemary Ellen. Guide to the Dark Side of the Paranormal. New Milford, Connecticut: Visionary Living, Inc., 2011

Hall, Judy. The Crystal Bible: A Definitive Guide to Crystals. Great Britain: Godsfield Press Ltd, 2003

Harner, Michael. The Way of the Shaman. HarperOne, 1990

Herr, Karl. Hex and Spellwork. Boston, MA/ York Beach, ME: Weiser Books, 2002

Hohman, John George. Pow-Wows or, Long Lost Friend. First published in 1820, and republished many times since.

Howe, Linda. How to Read the Akashic Records. Boulder, Colorado: Sounds True, 2009

Hunt, Stoker. Ouija: The Most Dangerous Game New York: Harper & Row Publishers, 1985

Hyatt, Harry Middleton. Folklore From Adams County Illinois. New York: Memoirs of the Alma Egan Hyatt Foundation, 1935

Hyatt, Harry Middleton. Hoodoo-Conjuration-Witchcraft-Rootwork: In Five Volumes, Volumes 1-5. Memoirs of the Alma Eagan Hyatt Foundation, 1935, 1965, 1970, 1973

Illes, Judika. Encyclopedia of Spirits: the ultimate guide to the magic of faries, genies, demons, ghosts, gods & goddesses. New York, NY: HarperCollins, 2009

Illes, Judika. Encyclopedia of Mystics, Saints, & Sages: A Guide to Asking for Protection, Wealth, Happiness, and Everything Else! . New York, NY: HarperCollins, 2011

Illes, Judika. Encyclopedia of 5000 Spells: the ultimate reference book for the magical arts. Hammersmith, London: Harper Element, 2004

Kowalewski, David Phd. Death Walkers: Shamanic Psychopomps, Earthbound Ghosts, and Helping Spirits in the Afterlife Realm. Bloomington, Indiana: iUniverse, 2015

Kuzmeskus, Elaine, M. Séance 101
Atglen, PA: Schiffer Publishing Ltd, 2007

Lerma, John, MD. Learning From the Light: Pre-Death Experiences, Prophecies, and Angelic Messages of Hope. Franklin Lakes, NJ: New Page Books, 2009

Livingston, John G. Adversaries Walk Among Us: A Guide to the Origin, Nature, and Removal of Demons and Spirits. Fort Bragg, CA: Lost Coast Press, 2004

Lynn, Heather, Phd. Evil Archeology: Demons, Possessions, and Sinister Relics. Newburyport, MA: Disinformation/Weiser Books, 2019

MacEowen, Frank. The Spiral of Memory and Belonging. New World Library, 2004

Madden, Kristin. Shamanic Guide to Death and Dying. St. Paul, Minnesota: Llewellyn Publications, 1999

Martin, Malachi. Hostage to the Devil: The Possession and Exorcism of Five Contemporary Americans. Harper San Francisco, 1976, 1992

Maurey, Eugene. Exorcism: How To Clear At A Distance A Spirit Possessed Person. West Chester Pennsylvania: Whitford Press, 1988

McCarthy, Josephine with McCarthy, Peter. The Exorcist's Handbook. Berkely, California: Golem Media, 2010

McCarthy, Josephine. Magical Knowledge: Book II The Initiate. Mandrake, 2011

McCarthy, Josephine. Magical Knowledge: Book III Contacts of the Adepts. Mandrake, 2012

McCoy, Edain. In a Graveyard at Midnight. St. Paul, MN: Llewellyn, 1995

Mc Teer, J. E.. Fifty Years As A Low Country Witch Doctor. Bloomington, IN: iUniverse, 1976, 1995, 2003, 2014 J.E. McTeer

Melody. Love is in the Earth: A Kaleidoscope of Crystals: The Reference Book Describing the Metaphysical Properties of the Mineral Kingdom. Earth Love Pub House, 1995

Mikaharic, Draja. Spiritual Cleansing: A Handbook of Psychic Self-Protection. San Francisco, California: Red Wheel/ Weiser, LLC, 1982, 2003

Mikaharic, Draja. Spiritual Worker's Spell Book. Xlibris Corp., 2002

Murray, Steve. Reiki: The Ultimate Guide Volume 4, Past Lives & Soul Retrieval. Las Vegas, NV: Body & Mind Productions, 2007

Northrop, Suzane with Kate McLoughlin. Séance: A Guide for the Living
Brooklyn, New York: Alliance Publishing, 1994

Penczak, Christopher. The Temple of Shamanic Witchcraft: Shadows, Spirits, and the Healing Journey. St. Paul, MN: Llewellyn Publications, 2005

Penczak, Christopher. The Magick of Reiki: Focused Energy for Healing, Ritual, & Spiritual Development. . Woodbury, MN: Llewellyn Publications, 2007

Penczak, Christopher. The Temple of High Witchcraft: Ceremonies, Spheres, and the Witches' Qabalah. Woodbury, MN: Llewellyn Publications, 2012

Pinckney, Roger. Blue Roots: African American folk Magic of the Gullah People. St. Paul, MN: Llewellyn Publications, 2000

Place, Robert M. A Gnostic Book of Saints. St. Paul MN: Llewellyn Publishing, 2001

Raines, Mary Elizabeth. The Laughing Cherub Guide to Past Life Regression: A Handbook for Real People. Sedona, AZ: Laughing Cherub Unlimited, 2010

Rysdyk, Evelyn C. Spirit Walking: A Course In Shamanic Power. San Francisco, CA, Red Wheel Weiser, LLC, 2013

Rogo, D. Scott and Bayless, Raymond. Phone Calls From The Dead: The results of a two-year investigation into an incredible phenomenon. Prentice-Hall, Inc., Englewood Cliffs, New Jersey, 1979

Salomone, Peter with Stephson, Robert. Shamanic Depossession: A Compassionate Healing Practice. Placerville, CA: Visione Sciamanica, 2014

Savedow, Steve. Sepher Rezial Hemelach: The Book of the Angel Rezial. York Beach, Maine: Samuel Weiser, Inc, 2000

Selig, Godfrey. Secrets of the Psalms. Published many times previously from author's handwritten journals; Create Space, 2014.

Shutan, Mary Mueller. The Spiritual Awakening Guide. Scotland, U.K.: Findhorn Press, 2015

Swain, BJ. Living Spirits: A Guide to Magic in a World of Spirits. Independently Published, 2018

Targ, Russell and Puthoff, Harold E. Mind – Reach: Scientists Look at Psychic AbilityUnited States: Delacorte Press, 1977

Taumaturgo, Agnostino. Christian Spiritual and Magical Rituals. THAVMA Publications

Telesco, Patricia. Ghosts, Spirits, and Hauntings. Freedom, California: The Crossing Press, 1999

Ullman M.D., Montague, Krippner Phd., Stanley, with Vaughan, Alan. Dream Telepathy: Experiments in Nocturnal Extrasensory Perception. Charlottesville, VA: Hampton Roads Publishing, 2002

W. Bill. Twelve Steps and Twelve Traditions. New York, NY: AA World Services, 1952

Warcollier, Rene`. Mind to Mind. Creative Age Press, 1948

Winkowski, Mary Ann. When Ghosts Speak: Understanding the World of Earthbound, Spirits.   New York, NY: Grand Central Publishing, 2007

Wood, Gail. The Shamanic Witch. San Francisco, CA: Weiser Books, 2008

Woodcroft, Ben. Angelic Sigils, Keys, & Calls. _ _ The Power of Magick Publishing, 2017

Yronwode, Catherine. Hoodoo Herb and Root Magic. Forestville, California: The Lucky Mojo Curio Company, 2002

Zweig, Connie Phd, and Wolf, Steve, Phd. Romancing the Shadow: A Guide to Soul Work for a Vital Authentic Life. New York: Ballentine Books/ Random House, 1997

Also see:

How Contacting the Dead Became a Family Game. Show on the Smithsonian Channel

Laura of The Paranormal Scholar Blog. Unmasking Zozo the Ouija Board Demon: The Making of a Modern Myth. Oct. 11, 2016

Printed in Great Britain
by Amazon